Teach Children Basic Bible Doctrine Using Pictures

RENÉE ELLISON

Published by Cross-Over
DBA Homeschool How-To's
Copyright 2013 by Renee Ellison
Website: http://www.homeschoolhowtos.com
Email: info@homeschoolhowtos.com

Library of Congress Cataloging-in-Publication Data
    Ellison, Renée, 1951-
        Teach children basic Bible doctrine using pictures/ Renée Ellison.
        Durango, Colo.: Homeschool How-To's, c2013.
        112 p.
        Previously published as A child's grip of Biblical doctrine ©1996 by Renée Ellison.
        Catechisms.
        Children--Religious life.
        Children--Conduct of life.
        Bible--Theology.
        Theology, Doctrinal--Popular works.
        ISBN-10: 0988283573
        ISBN-13: 978-0-9882835-7-2

All rights reserved. No part of this publication may be reproduced, stored in a retrieval system, or transmitted in any form or by any means—for example, elec-tronic, photocopy, or recording—without the prior written permission of the publisher. The only exception is brief quotations.

However, this is reproducible: Whoever purchases this book has permission to photocopy its pages for non-commercial use by family or classes.

Cover design by Erin Jones of Piebird Creative.

Printed in the United States of America.

Teach children basic Bible doctrine, using pictures. ~ 30 lessons ~

A child's grip of biblical doctrine

A picture workbook of the great themes and concepts of the Bible

<u>Yesterday</u>'s children knew the Westminster Catechism by heart, and could answer over 100 questions regarding our faith. Their foundation was rock solid.

<u>Today</u>'s children tend to be blown about by every wind of doctrine. They may have heard many Bible stories, but they don't know how those stories all fit together, and most couldn't tell you the core unshakable beliefs of Christianity.

These easy 30 fill-in-the-blank lessons, for students from the 4th grade up, cover all the basic doctrines of our faith, giving our children the same stable Biblical framework their ancestors had.

Sample questions:
1. What is the chief end of man?
2. Tell how Christ functions as Prophet, Priest, and King.
3. Define omniscient, omnipotent, and omnipresent.
4. What is the ninth commandment?

Children who have been trained in this course will know the answers to these questions and scores of others like them.

To get started, read this section first: **how to use this book (page 3).**

Table of Contents

30 lessons for teaching children basic Bible doctrine, using pictures:

To get started, read page 3 first: how to use this book

Knowing Doctrine (p. 4)

1. What is the chief end of man? (p. 4)
2. What is salvation? (p. 8)
3. How to win souls (p. 12)
4. Keep your life on the right track (p. 21)
5. God is... (p. 25)
    - ...omnipotent
    - ...omnipresent
    - ...omniscient
6. The concept of the Trinity (p. 27)
7. God, the Creator (p. 30)
8. Christ: Prophet, Priest and King (p. 33)
9. The Holy Spirit: description, gifts and offices, and fruit (p. 35)
10. Two Christian sacraments: Baptism and communion (p. 41)
11. The Ten Commandments (p. 43)
12. The Lord's Prayer (p. 47)
13. Development of the concept of sacrificial atonement in Biblical history (p. 51)
14. The Tabernacle (p. 53)
15. The Apostles' Creed (p. 55)
16. The Heidelberg Catechism; Bible pledge of allegiance (p. 57)
17. Judgments, rewards, & crowns (p. 61)

Practicing Overcoming (p. 65)

18. The enemy (p. 65)
19. The believer's armor (p. 67)
20. How to overcome temptation (p. 74)
21. Choosing wise companions (p. 77)
22. How love acts: 1 Corinthians 13 (p. 79)
23. We lack nothing: Psalm 23 (p. 81)
24. Obedience (p. 85)
25. Faith vs. good works (p. 89)

Grasping the Bible (p. 93)

26. The inspired book (p. 95)
27. One-minute survey (p. 97)
28. Old Testament books (p. 100)
29. New Testament books (p. 107)
30. Find a verse in 10 seconds (p. 110)

HOW TO USE THIS BOOK

> The pages in this book are reproducible for the people in your domain. Whoever purchases this book has permission to photocopy its pages for non-commercial use by their family and/or in classes they teach.

1. Show your child each page (the ones with empty blanks are for the student; the filled-in pages are for the teacher),
    A. To engage the child's interest in the topic and
    B. To heighten awareness of what he does not already know.

2. Then take away the page of empty blanks.

3. Pull out the answer page (which only you as the teacher see) and teach all of the concepts on that page. Have your child listen very attentively, telling him ahead of time that he will hear the answers to all those questions that were on the first page you showed him.

4. Then return the page with the empty blanks and have him answer as many as he can by himself.

5. Finally, work through the rest of the blanks until the page is completed.

6. Review the lesson from the day before, before beginning each day's new lesson.

Or, use this workbook for older children to teach themselves. They could study the answer pages first, and then fill in the blanks pages without looking at the answer sheets.

Either way, this manual's exposure to the major themes of scripture will give your child a grasp of Christianity that will serve him all his life.

Lesson 1: What is the chief end (= purpose, reason for living) of man?

To _____ God and _____ Him forever.

Glorify

_____ God, like He _____ us.

Be in tune with God. Do what He wants of you, every waking moment.

___ resistance; ___ delay; ___ rebellion; ___ protest. Only _____!

Isaiah 43:7 "Everyone who is called by my name, and whom I have _____ for _____ _____."

Isaiah 43:21 "The people whom I _____ for _____ will declare my praise."

Proverbs 11:30 "He who is _____ _____ souls."

Daniel 12:3 "Those who lead _____ to righteousness will _____ like the stars forever."

Matthew 28:19-20 "Go therefore and _____ disciples of ____ nations."
☞ send money
☞ pray
☞ go yourself

Enjoy

_____ in Him;
_____ and _____ with Him.
_____ Him; _____ in Him;
_____ Him; _____ Him.

Finish
glorify
enjoy

all else will _____, _____, _____

Lesson 1: What is the chief end (= purpose, reason for living) of man?

(answer page)

To *glorify* God and *enjoy* Him forever.

Glorify

Serve God, like He *serves* us.

Be in tune with God. Do what He wants of you, every waking moment.

No resistance; *no* delay;
no rebellion; *no* protest.
Only *yes*!

Isaiah 43:7 "Everyone who is called by my name, and whom I have *created* for *my glory*."

Isaiah 43:21 "The people whom I *formed* for *myself* will declare my praise."

Proverbs 11:30 "He who is *wise wins* souls."

Daniel 12:3 "Those who lead *many* to righteousness will *shine* like the stars forever."

Matthew 28:19-20 "Go therefore and *make* disciples of *all* nations."
- send money
- pray
- go yourself

Enjoy

Confide in Him;
play and *work* with Him.
Worship Him; *delight* in Him;
thank Him; *love* Him.

Some people live to…

1
have _____.
--to be protected from everything that might go wrong

2
have _____.
"been there, done that"
--going to the moon, save the earth; the Arctic, bottom of the ocean; climb tall mountains; travel

3
have _____.
--living to right wrongs; to re-shape practices of societies; to clean or organize things; save the earth, animals

4
be _____
or get _____
--terrorists, hijackers, avengers
--goal: to kill the most people; blow up the biggest building…
--cults, gangs, the occult

5
have _____;
indulge _____.
--food, music, movies, drugs, soap operas, pornography, pulp novels, retirement; maximum comfort and luxury with the least amount of work

6
_____
--wanting to do a skill over and over, because you're good at it: inventing, writing, building…

7
gain
_____
--education: to know more; to earn more and more degrees
--Leonardo da Vinci searched for salvation through knowledge

but none of these is the ultimate reason to live…

8
have _____ / take ____
--acquiring lots of things
--gambling; video games
--have _____; do risky or daring things; bungee jumping; ice swimming

9
_____ _____
--to be one of the most beautiful human specimens around

10
have _____
--wanting the entire world to do as I say
--wanting to be the _____ at something: Olympic gold; Nobel Prize; greatest musician

11
have _____ _____
--wanting a family dynasty; popularity; a million friends; fame; living vicariously through others (rock stars, children)

Some people live to... *(answer page)*

1 have *security*
--to be protected from everything that might go wrong

2 have *experiences*
"been there, done that"
--going to the moon, save the earth; the Arctic, bottom of the ocean; climb tall mountains; travel

3 have *causes*
--living to right wrongs; to re-shape practices of societies; to clean or organize things; save the earth, animals

4 be *rebellious* or get *attention*
--terrorists, hijackers, avengers
--goal: to kill the most people; blow up the biggest building…
--cults, gangs, the occult

5 have *pleasure* indulge *fantasies*
--food, music, movies, drugs, soap operas, pornography, pulp novels, retirement; maximum comfort and luxury with the least amount of work

6 *produce*
--wanting to do a skill over and over, because you're good at it: inventing, writing, building…

7 gain *knowledge*
--education: to know more; to earn more and more degrees
--Leonardo da Vinci searched for salvation through knowledge

8 have *money*/ take *risks*
--acquiring lots of things
--gambling; video games
--have _____; do risky or daring things; bungee jumping; ice swimming

9 *look good*
--to be one of the most beautiful human specimens around

10 have *control*
--wanting the entire world to do as I say
--wanting to be the _____ at something: Olympic gold; Nobel Prize; greatest musician

11 have *human love*
--wanting a family dynasty; popularity; a million friends; fame; living vicariously through others (rock stars, children)

but none of these is the ultimate reason to live…

Lesson 2: What is salvation?

GOD:
- God _____ you.
- God _____ you.
- God is _____.
- He wants you to _____ in heaven with _____.
- But there is one thing that can never be in heaven: _____.

SIN:
- All people have _____ -- even _____, the mother of Jesus.
- Sin is "___" in the middle (S-I-N); putting _____ first.
- Sin is anything we ____, _____, or _____ that is not pleasing to God. "Your iniquities have made a separation between ____ and your ___." (Isaiah 59:2)
- When we break even _____ commandment, we're guilty of breaking all ten, because we've broken God's perfect law.
- The first commandment _____ is impossible for anyone to _____: to love the Lord with _____ of your strength.
- **There is some pull in us that wants to ignore God, to be callous toward Him, to have a _____ in our hearts. We are sluggish to _____ Him. The words of an old hymn remind us that we are "Prone to wander, Lord, I _____ it; prone to _____ the God I love."**

Lesson 2: What is salvation? *(answer page)*

GOD:
- God *made* you.
- God *loves* you.
- God is *perfect*.
- He wants you to *live* in heaven with *Him*.
- But there is one thing that can never be in heaven: *sin*.

SIN:
- All people have *sinned*-- even *Mary*, the mother of Jesus.
- Sin is "*I*" in the middle (S-I-N); putting *self* first.
- Sin is anything we *do*, *say*, or *think* that is not pleasing to God.

  "Your iniquities have made a separation between *you* and your *God*." (Isaiah 59:2)

- When we break even *one* commandment, we're guilty of breaking all ten, because we've broken God's perfect law.
- The first commandment *alone* is impossible for anyone to *keep*: to love the Lord with *all* of your strength.

  There is some pull in us that wants to ignore God, to be callous toward Him, to have a *hardness* in our hearts. We are sluggish to *obey* Him.

  The words of an old hymn remind us that we are "Prone to wander, Lord, I *feel* it; prone to *leave* the God I love."

SIN: People are _____ sinful, just as dogs are born with a _____ in them. We have a *propensity* to sin; we _____ in that direction.

If Adam and Eve hadn't fallen into sin, ____ would have!

COST: The cost of sin is _____. You can't _____ yourself.

THE SAVIOR: The **gospel** means _____ _____.

The Messiah willingly died for _____ sins and came back to _____ again.

Because He was _____, He is the _____ one who could _____ for us and have it accomplish _____ for us.

There is only _____ Savior.

Acts 4:12: There is salvation in ____ _____ name.
Isa. 45:21: There is no _____ besides _____.
Isa. 45:5: I am the _____, and there is _____ other.

RECEIVE HIS GIFT: We don't _____ this gift. We receive it. Like _____ in the _____, it's useless unless we withdraw it. The Messiah made a _____ for you to be saved from _____, but it isn't yours until you _____ out and accept ____.

It's as simple as ___, ___, ___:

Admit that you are a sinner and can_____ save yourself.

Believe that the Savior died and rose again for _____ sin.

Choose to receive Him as your Savior _____.

SIN: People are *born* sinful, just as dogs are born with a *bark* in them.

We have a *propensity* to sin; we *lean* in that direction.

If Adam and Eve hadn't fallen into sin, *we* would have!

COST: The cost of sin is *death*. You can't *save* yourself.

THE SAVIOR: The **gospel** means *good news*.

The Messiah willingly died for *your* sins and came back to *life* again.

Because He was *perfect*, He is the *only* one who could *die* for us and have it accomplish *forgiveness* for us.

There is only *one* Savior.

Acts 4:12: "There is salvation in *no other* name."

Isa. 45:21: "There is no *God* besides Me."

Isa. 45:5: "I am the *Lord*, and there is *no* other.

RECEIVE HIS GIFT: We don't *earn* this gift. We receive it. Like *money* in the *bank*, it's useless unless we withdraw it. The Messiah made a *way* for you to be saved from *hell*, but it isn't yours until you *reach* out and accept *it*.

It's as simple as *A, B, C*:

Admit that you are a sinner and can*not* save yourself.

Believe that the Savior died and rose again for *your* sin.

Choose to receive Him as your Savior *today*.

Lesson 3: How to win souls

Poem to use with the "Gospel in Colors" booklet

My sin is as black as black can be.
It will spoil heaven, said He.

So He covered it up with His own blood red.
Christ took my place on a cross and bled.

He made me all so clean and white;
like a star I'll shine, forever bright,

And go to live where streets are gold.
I'll be with Him for days untold.

And now I grow all strong and green,
Believing in Him, who I've never seen.

I feed on His word to learn what's right,
And rest in His promises day and night.

How to use this poem in a booklet:

This poem accompanies the booklet that the children make (described on the following page). The patterns are for making three booklets from one sheet of paper. So, if you have 12 children, you only have to make 4 photocopies. Have the children color in the squares and fold the book back and forth like a fan. Then staple one edge so that it functions like a book, with pages to turn.

black	black	red	red	white	white	gold	gold

green on back of this square → ← green on back of this square

---

black	black	red	red	white	white	gold	gold

green on back of this square → ← green on back of this square

---

black	black	red	red	white	white	gold	gold

green on back of this square → ← green on back of this square

Winning souls:
Salvation in a nutshell

1. Everyone sins.

2. The cost of sin is death.

   Yeshua
3. Jesus paid the cost for us.

4. If you **trust and obey Him,** you shall have eternal life.

Draw on the blackboard and talk about how <u>simple</u> salvation is.

Explanation of the Gospel picture stories (on the following page) **to use when leading others to Christ:**

1. **Jump across the Atlantic Ocean.** Suppose I have a neighbor who always lives very unselfishly--much better than I do. She *appears* to be more holy than other humans, but she still is far less holy than God is. If she and I both jump into the Atlantic Ocean, she may jump further than I do, but her leap still falls woefully short of reaching the other shore.

2. **There is truly only one way to achieve some things in life.** You can't roller skate your way to the moon; you can only get there by a rocket. There aren't several answers to one math problem. Similarly, there are not <u>many</u> ways to God--through Buddha, Mohammed, etc.--as people who follow New Age religions might suggest. There is only <u>one</u> way to God--through Christ. Other ways to heaven just aren't available.

3. If someone **assumed the punishment that was intended for you** (for example, taking your death sentence in a gas chamber for a deadly crime you committed), you would be a changed person forever.

A picture approach to sharing the Gospel:

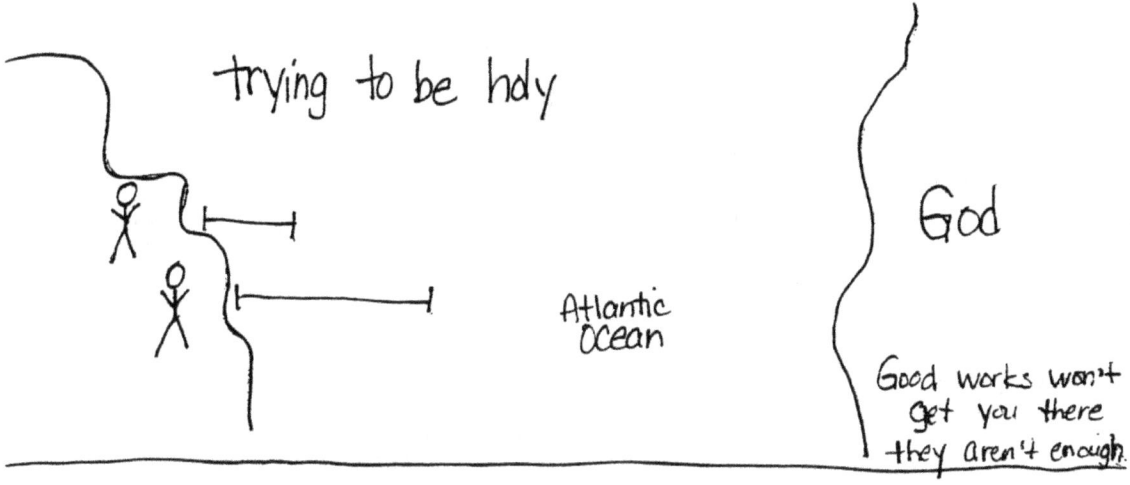

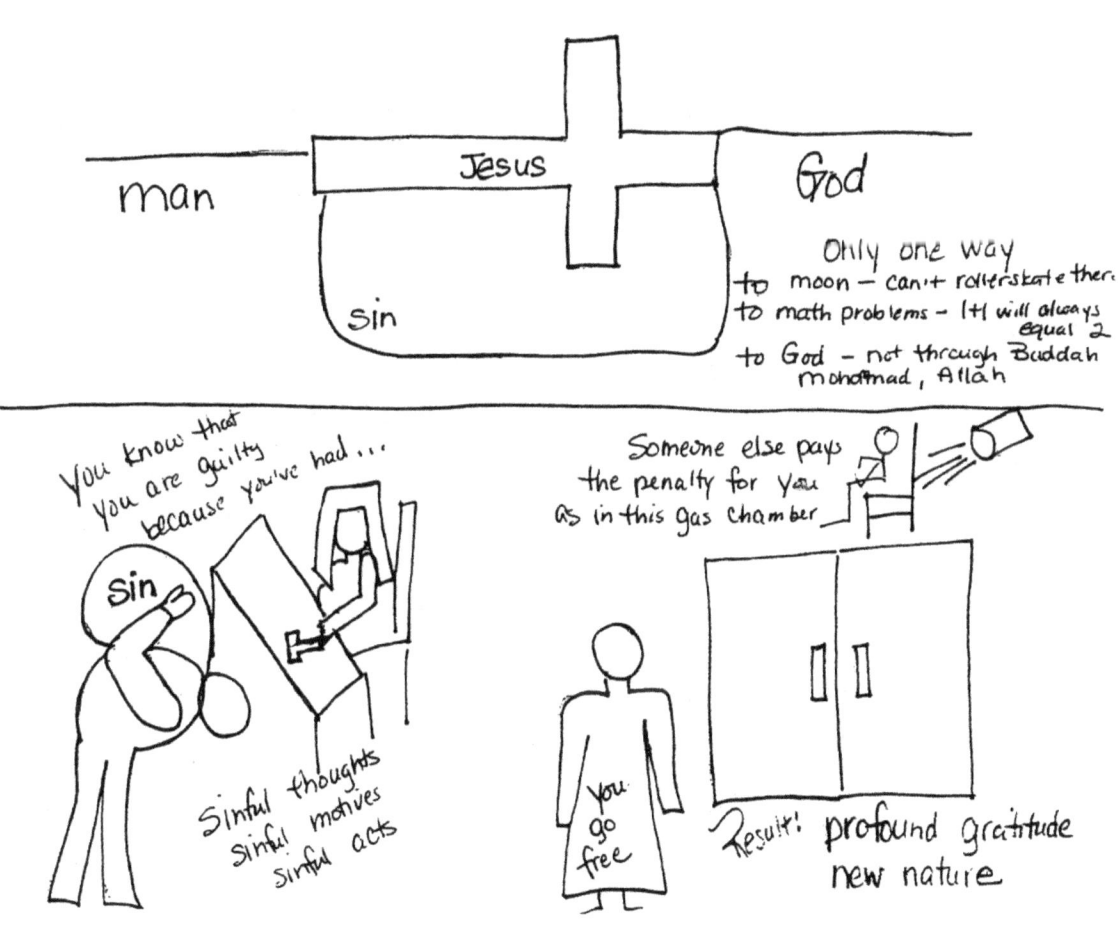

Salvation verses to use in leading souls to the Messiah:

Romans 3:23
...for all have sinned and fall short of the glory of God.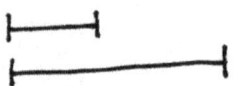

Romans 6:23
For the wages of sin is death, but the free gift of God is eternal life in Christ Jesus our Lord.

John 3:16
For God so loved the world that He gave His only begotten Son, that whoever believes in Him should not perish but have eternal life.

John 3:36
He who believes in the Son has eternal life; but He who does not obey the Son shall not see life, but the wrath of God abides on him.

Romans 10:9
If you confess with your mouth Jesus as Lord, and believe in your heart that God raised Him from the dead, you shall be saved.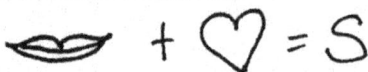

Salvation verses:

> He who believes in the Son has eternal life; but he who does not obey the Son shall not see life, but the wrath of God abides on him.
> _____

> ...for all have sinned and fall short of the glory of God...
> _____

> For God so loved the world that He gave His only begotten Son, that whoever believes in Him should not perish, but have eternal life.
> _____

> If you confess with your mouth Jesus as Lord, and believe in your heart that God raised Him from the dead, you shall be saved.
> _____

> For the wages of sin is death but the free gift of God is eternal life in Christ Jesus our Lord
>
> Verse name: _____
> Picture:

Put the verse names and pictures into the boxes above

Match 'em up!

John 3:16 -- Romans 10:9 -- Romans 3:23 -- John 3:36 -- Romans 6:23

Salvation verses:

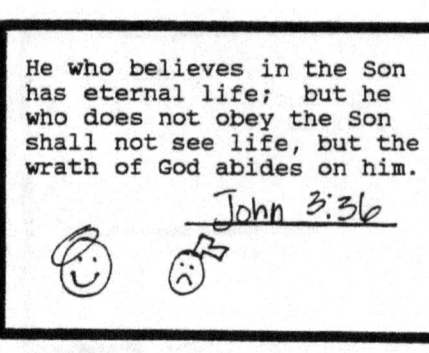

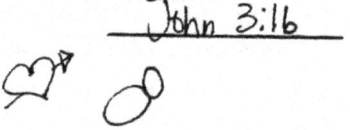

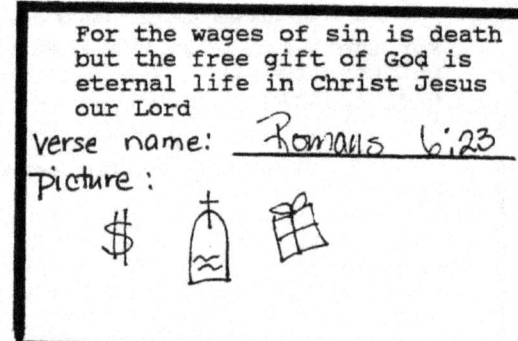

Put these verse names and pictures into the boxes above

Match 'em up!

John 3:16 -- Romans 10:9 -- Romans 3:23 --John 3:36--Romans 6:23

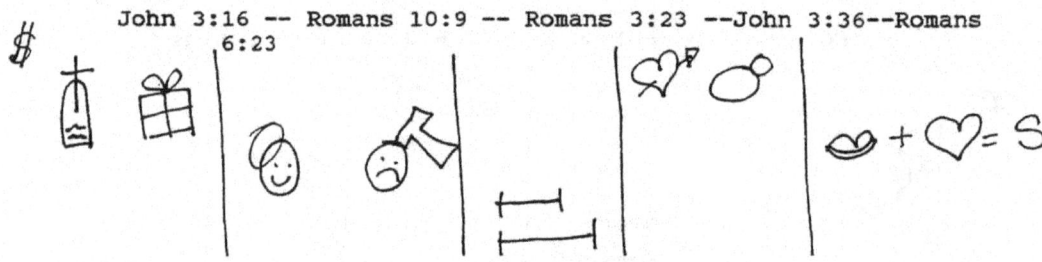

Complete these verses by choosing the correct numbers from the list of phrases at the bottom:

…For all have sinned _____

For the wages of sin is death _____

For God so loved the world _____

He who believes in the son has eternal life; _____

If you confess with your mouth Jesus (Yeshua) as Lord _____

Select the correct phrase(s) from the following list to complete the above verses:

__1.__ but he who does not obey the Son shall not see life,

__2.__ but the free gift of God is eternal life in Christ Jesus our Lord

__3.__ and believe in your heart that God raised him from the dead

__4.__ that He gave His only begotten son

__5.__ and fall short of the glory of God

__6.__ but the wrath of God abides on Him

__7.__ that whoever believes in Him should not perish,

__8.__ you shall be saved

__9.__ but have eternal life

Finish these verses
by choosing the correct numbers from the bottom list of phrases

…For all have sinned __5.__

For the wages of sin is death __2.__

For God so loved the world ___4., 7., 9.__

He who believes in the son has eternal life; ___1., 6.__

If you confess with your mouth Jesus (Yeshua) as Lord ___3., 8.__

Select the correct phrase(s) from this list to complete the above verses:

__1.__ but he who does not obey the Son shall not see life,

__2.__ but the free gift of God is eternal life in Christ Jesus our Lord

__3.__ and believe in your heart that God raised him from the dead

__4.__ that He gave His only begotten son

__5.__ and fall short of the glory of God

__6.__ but the wrath of God abides on Him

__7.__ that whoever believes in Him should not perish,

__8.__ you shall be saved

__9.__ but have eternal life

Lesson 4: How to keep your life on THE RIGHT TRACK

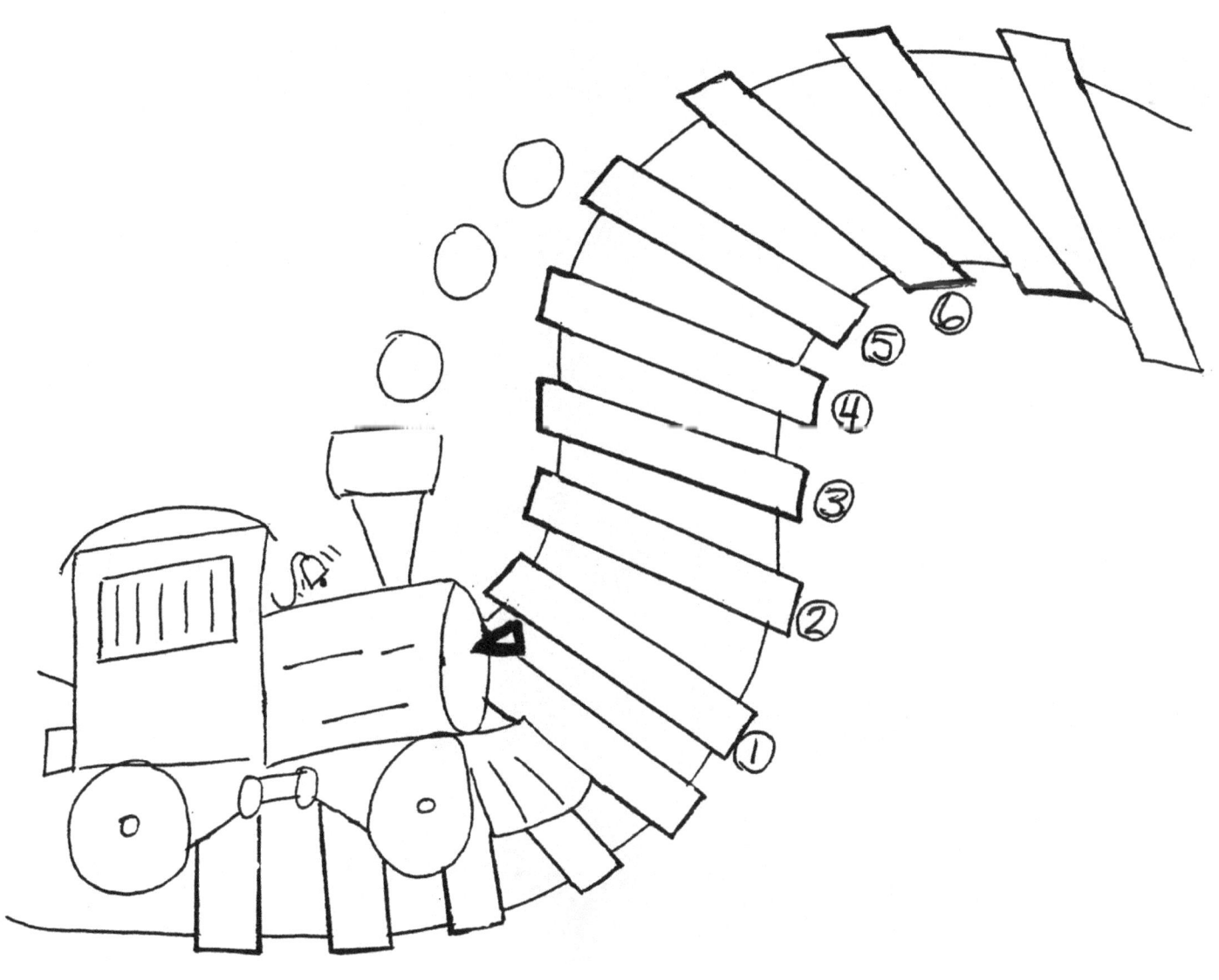

Lesson 4: How to keep your life on THE RIGHT TRACK (answer page)

Bible
entire hand clutches the Bible

Prayer
A_____

C_____

T_____

S_____

Evangelism

Tell others with your

_____ and

with your _____.

Fellowship

"Do not _____ to _____ together, as is the _____ of some" (Heb. 10:25).

We receive two sermons at church:
1. From the _____.
2. From the lives of _____ _____.

Tithe

Giving the first of your _____ by giving the first _____ of your money.

Figure the tithe by dropping the last _____.

The tithe is only the _____ point. One person gave 9/10ths and only kept 1/10th for his own personal use.

All that we have…is _____'s.

Love of God and _____

Love the Lord your God with
____ your heart
____ your strength
____ your mind
and love your neighbor as
_____

(answer page)

Bible
entire hand clutches the Bible

- read
- listen
- meditate
- memorize
- do

Prayer

Adoration

Confession

Thanksgiving

Supplication

Evangelism

Tell others with your *behavior* and with your *words*.

Fellowship

"Do not *neglect* to *meet* together, as is the *habit* of some" (Heb. 10:25).

We receive two sermons at church:
1. From the *pulpit*.
2. From the lives of *other believers*.

Tithe

Giving the first of your *time* by giving the first *tenth* of your money.

Figure the tithe by dropping the last *number*.

The tithe is only the *starting* point. One person gave 9/10ths and only kept 1/10th for his own personal use.

All that we have…is *God*'s.

Love of God and *others*

Love the Lord your God with
- *all* your heart
- *all* your strength
- *all* your mind

and love your neighbor as *yourself*

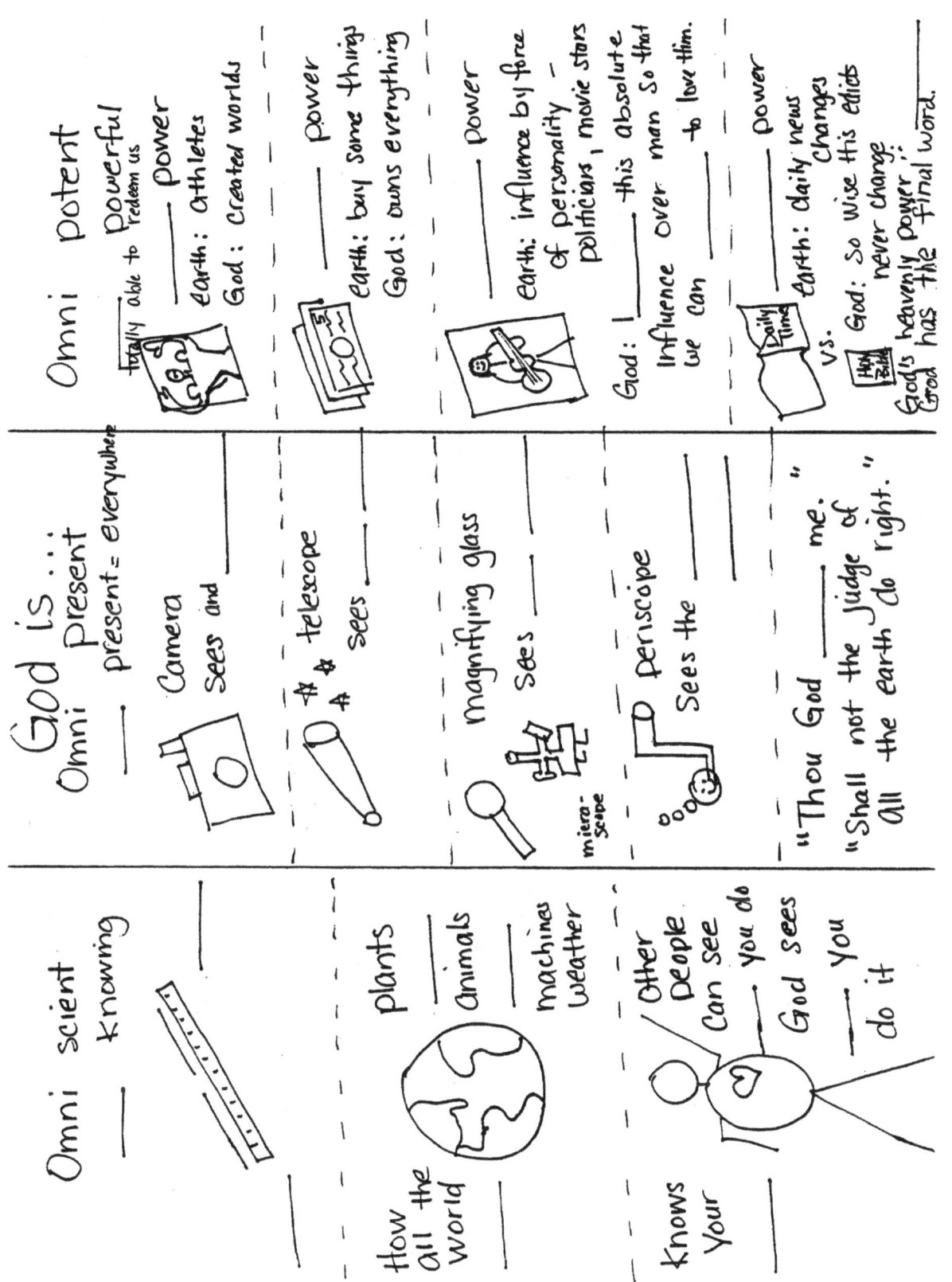

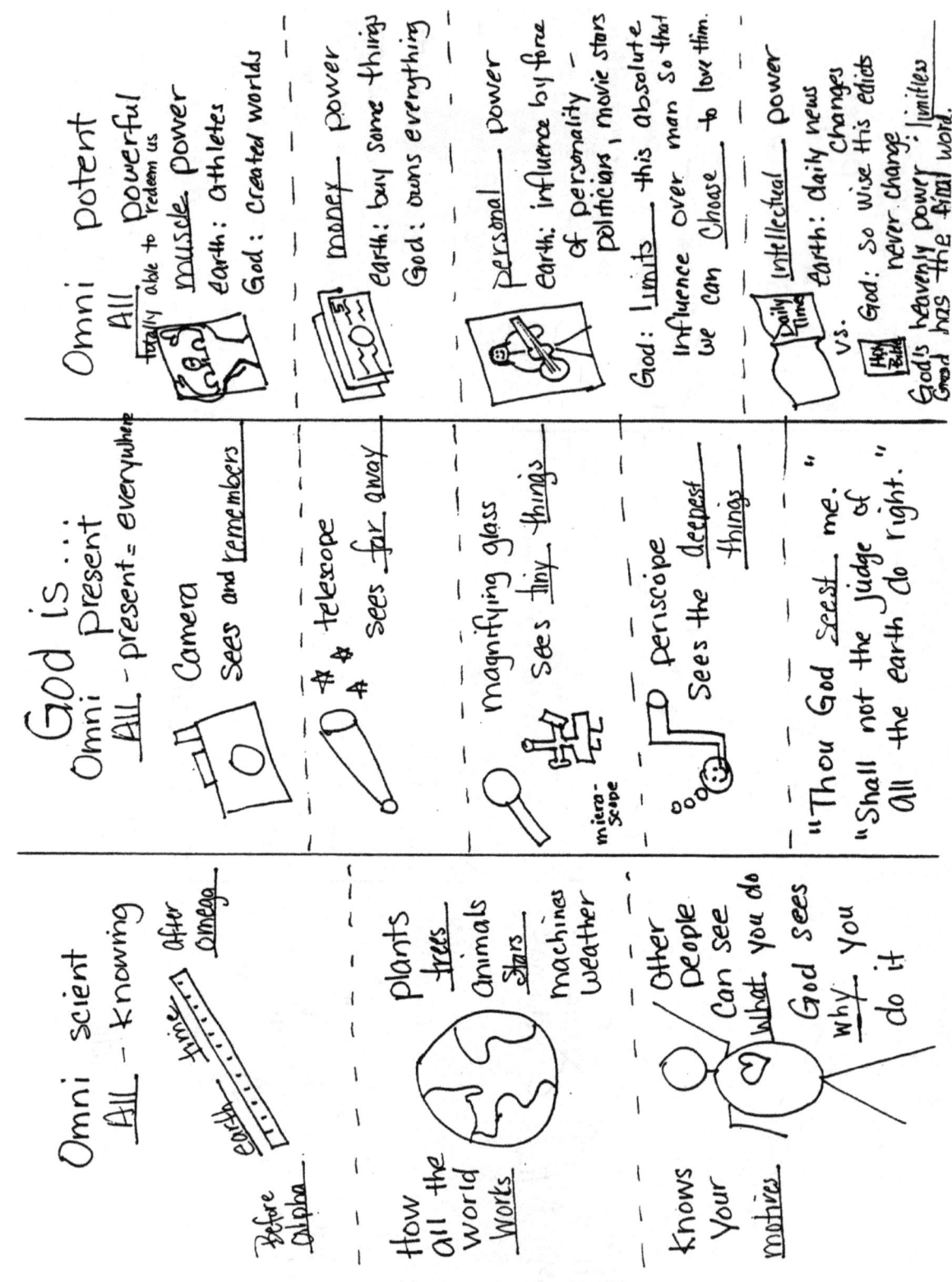

26

Lesson 6: The concept of the Trinity

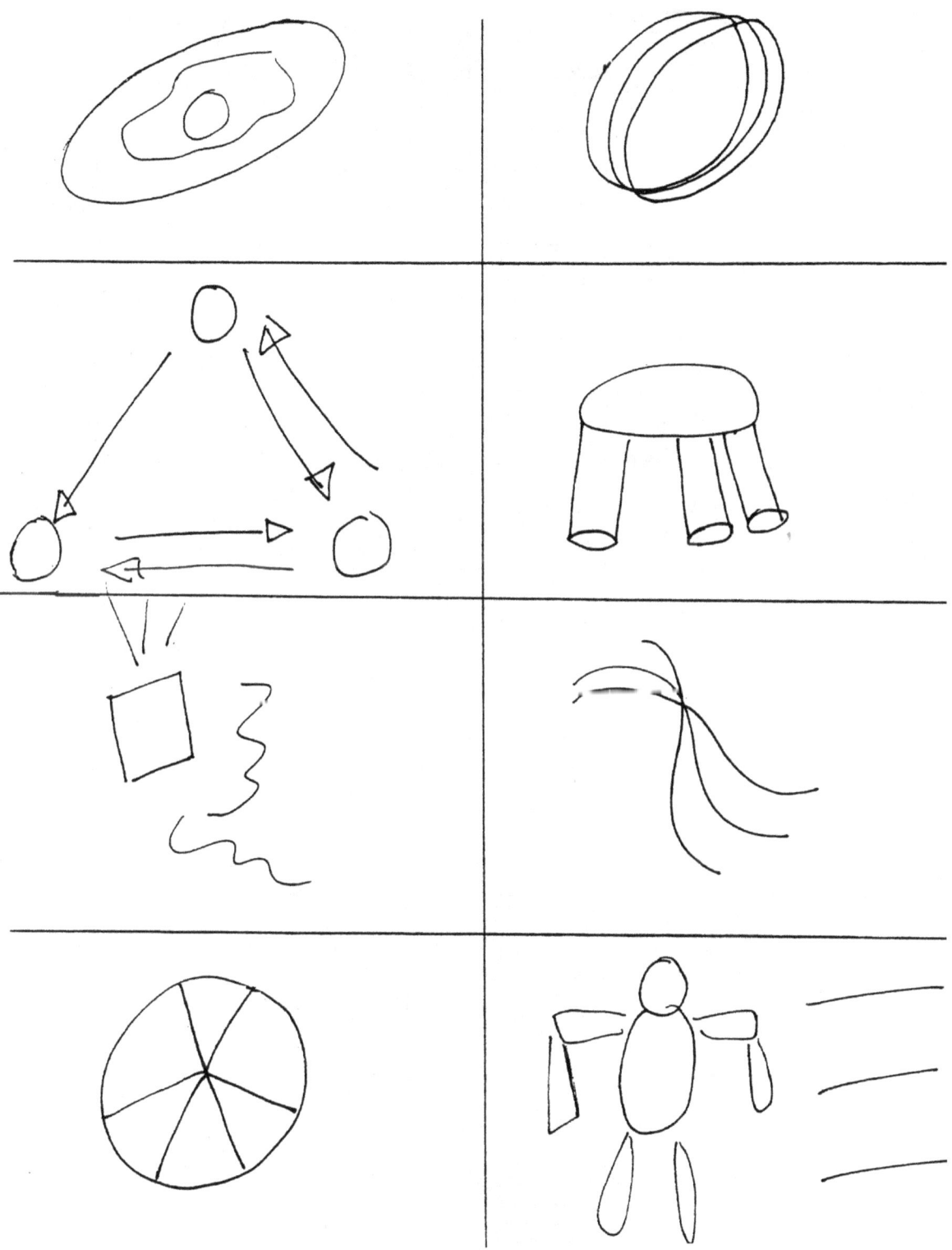

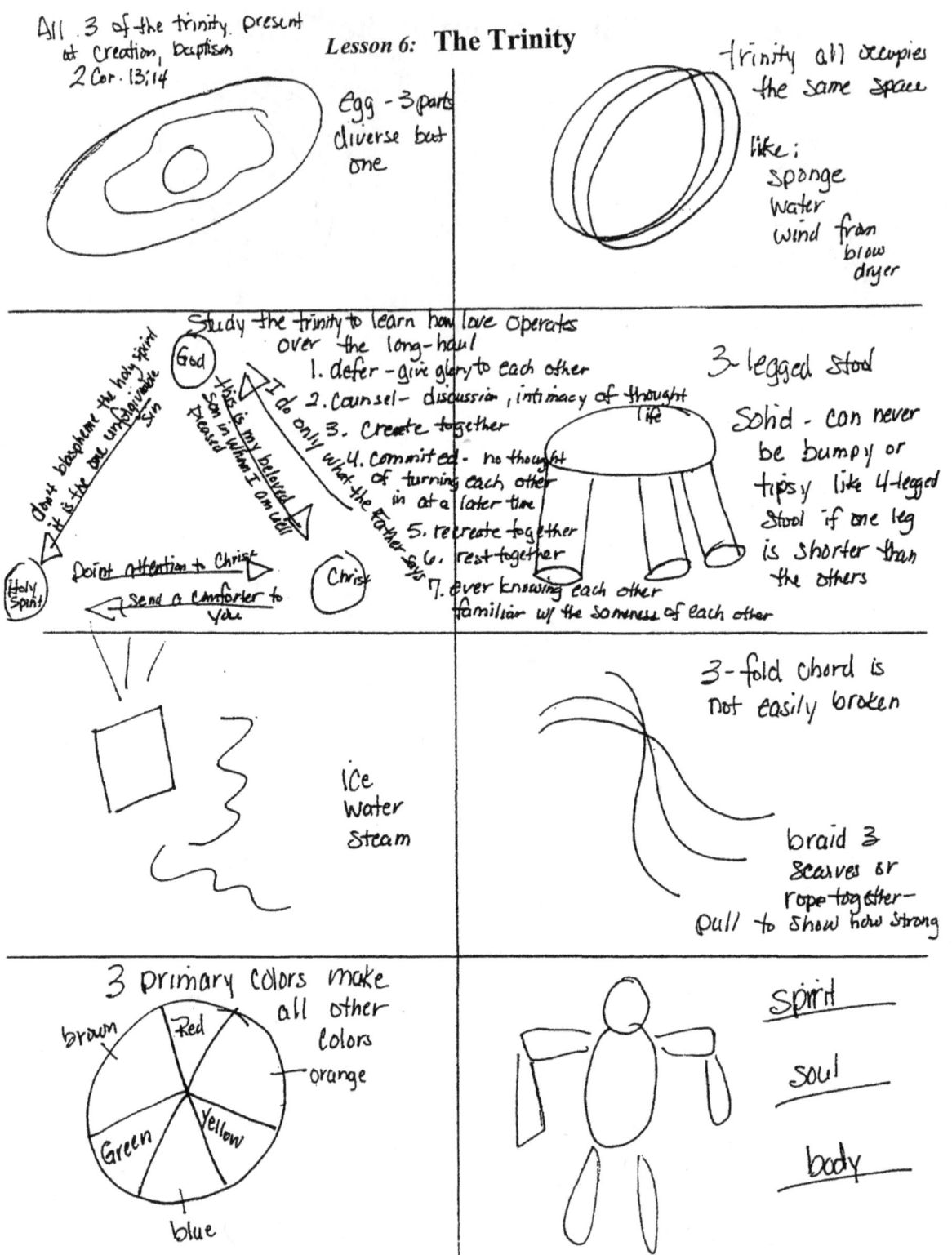

Lesson 7: God, the Creator

His creation

day   **activity**

1. God separated the light from the darkness.

2. Waters in heaven;
   waters on earth.

3. Dry land, plants and trees;
   sea.

4. Sun, moon, and stars.

5. Water animals;
   birds.

6. Land animals;
   man: Adam and Eve.

7. Sabbath rest.

Lesson 8: Messiah/Christ: The Prophet, Priest and King

Prophet

1. Announces coming events _____ _____.
2. Warns people of _____.
3. Encourages people to get their _____.
4. Makes people _____ something. They can't be _____ or ride the _____.
5. Tells people the true state of the world—not just what everyone _____.

A prophet often looks like this:
- Doesn't have nice clothes or a place to lay his head.
- Doesn't care what people think or do.
- Threw Jeremiah into a _____.
- Cut off John the Baptist's _____.

Luke 7:16: A great _____ has appeared among us, and God has visited His people.

Luke 24:19: Jesus…was a _____ mighty in deed and word in the sight of _____ and all the _____.

Priest

sinful man — go-between — Holy God
offers sacrifices for

1. A _____ _____. Without the shedding of _____ there is no remission of _____.
2. Offers _____.
3. Christ offered _____, once and for all, an eternal sacrifice.
4. He prays for _____. He always lives to make intercession for us. (Hebrews 7:25)
5. He was without _____, after the order of Melchizedek.

Hebrews 6:20: He has become a high _____ forever.

Hebrews 7:25: He is able to save _____ those who _____ to God.

King

1. Rules with absolute _____; doesn't appeal to anyone else.
2. Solves _____.
3. Declares _____.
4. His subjects serve Him and _____ Him.
5. He declares events & celebrations.
6. He builds beautiful _____.
7. He gives gift of _____, position, and opportunities to loyal subjects.

Rev. 17:14: King of _____ and Lord of _____.

Psalm 44:4: You are my King and my _____.

Luke 23:38: The _____ of the Jews.

John 18:37: "So you are a _____?" "You say _____ that I am a King."

33

Lesson 8: Messiah/Christ: The Prophet, Priest and King *(answer page)*

Prophet

Priest

King

sinful man   go-between   Holy God

Prophet

1. Announces coming events *before* they *happen*.
2. Warns people of *judgment*.
3. Encourages people to get their *hearts right*.
4. Makes people *decide* something. They can't be *lukewarm* or ride the *fence*.
5. Tells people the true state of the world—not just what everyone *sees*.

A prophet often looks like this:
- Doesn't have nice clothes or a place to lay his head.
- Doesn't care what people think or do.
- Threw Jeremiah into a *well*.
- Cut off John the Baptist's *head*.

Luke 7:16: A great *prophet* has appeared among us, and God has visited His people.

Luke 24:19: Jesus…was a *prophet* mighty in deed and word in the sight of *God* and all the people.

Priest

1. A *priest* offers sacrifices for *sins*.
2. Offers *blood*. Without the shedding of *blood* there is no remission of *sins*.
3. Christ offered *Himself*, once and for all, an eternal sacrifice.
4. He prays for *you*. He always lives to make intercession for us. (Hebrews 7:25)
5. He was without *father*, after the order of Melchizedek.

Hebrews 6:20: He has become a high *priest* forever.

Hebrews 7:25: He is able to save *forever* those who *draw near* to God.

King

1. Rules with absolute *authority* doesn't appeal to anyone else.
2. Solves *problems*.
3. Declares *war*.
4. His subjects serve Him and *honor* Him.
5. He declares events and celebrations.
6. He builds beautiful *places*.
7. He gives gift of *money*, position, and opportunities to loyal subjects.

Rev. 17:14: King of *kings* and Lord of *lords*.

Psalm 44:4: You are my King and my *God*.

Luke 23:38: The King of the Jews.

John 18:37: "So you are a King?" "You say correctly that I am a *King*."

34

Lesson 9: The Holy Spirit: Who He is, and 7 things He does

Who? ____ person of the Trinity
We can't _____ Him.
Symbol of the _____.
The one unforgivable ____ is
   blaspheming Him.
He doesn't draw attention to _____
   but gives _____ to the Father and to
   the Son (John 16:14).
	(4) Convicts of _____.
	Exposes other people's ___;
	   makes it _____.
	_____ you _____ to do
	   the sin that is tempting
	   you at the moment.
	Brings to your mind _____ sins
	   that you've already committed, that
	   you need to _____ of.
	        {Object lesson: flashlight.}

(1) _____
You were _____ for the day of
   redemption (Eph. 4:30).
      {Object lesson: envelope.}
	(5) _____ →
	You'll hear a voice behind you, saying
	   "This ___ the _____; walk ye in it."
	      {Object lesson: arrow.}

(2) _____-_____
He was _____ on O.T.
   people. Now He _____ us all
   the time.
"I will baptize you with the
   _____ _____ and
   with _____."
{Object lesson: glass of water.}
	(6) _____ **with boldness**
	"…but you shall receive
	   ____ when the _____
	   _____.has come
	   upon you" (Acts 1:8).
	   {Object lesson: electric fan blowing.}

(3) _____ (_____)
Jesus said He would
   give you another
   _____, that He
   may be _____
   _____ forever.
(Helps you solve the
situation, no to judge it.)
{Object: blanket.}
	(7) _____
	"He will ____ you all things" (John 14:26)
	"and bring to remembrance all that I
	   said ___ _____."
	The words of the Bible can lay on the
	   page or can leap up and shape your
	   life—hot-wired. He makes the
	   _____ come _____.
	   {Object lesson: chalk.}

Lesson 9: The Holy Spirit: Who He is, and 7 things He does:
(answer page)

Who? *3rd* **person of the Trinity** We can't *see* Him. Symbol of the *dove*. The one unforgivable *sin* is blaspheming Him. He doesn't draw attention to *Himself* but gives *glory* to the Father and to the Son (John 16:14).	**(4) Convicts of *sin*** Exposes other people's *sin*; makes it *public*. *Warns* you *not* to do the sin that is tempting you at the moment. Brings to your mind *specific sins* that you've already committed, that you need to repent of. {Object lesson: flashlight.}
(1) *Seals* You were *sealed* for the day of redemption (Eph. 4:30). {Object lesson: envelope.}	**(5) *Counsels* →** You'll hear a voice behind you, saying "This *is* the *way*; walk ye in it." {Object lesson: arrow.}
(2) *Indwells - fills* He was *sometimes* on O.T. people. Now He *indwells* us all the time. "I will baptize you with the *Holy Spirit* and with *fire*." {Object lesson: glass of water.}	**(6) *Empowers* with boldness** "...but you shall receive *power* when the *Holy Spirit* has come upon you" (Acts 1:8). {Object lesson: electric fan blowing.}
(3) *Comforts (Companion)* Jesus said He would give you another *Helper*, that He may be *with you* forever. (Helps you solve the situation, no to judge it.) {Object: blanket.}	**(7) *Teaches*** "He will *teach* you all things" (John 14:26) "and bring to remembrance all that I said *to you*." The words of the Bible can lay on the page or can leap up and shape your life—hot-wired. He makes the *Bible* come *alive*. {Object lesson: chalk.}

Gifts and offices of the Holy Spirit:

God's gift to us...

How much _____ shall your _____ father give the _____ _____ to those who _____ him.
Luke 11:13

↓

Spirit gives →
_____
_____

Gifts of the Spirit

1. [ ]
2. [ ]
3. [ ]
4. [ ]
5. [ ]
6. [ ]
7. [ ]
8. [ ]
9. [ ]

Offices of the Spirit

① _____
② _____
③ _____
④ _____
⑤ _____

Gifts and offices of the Holy Spirit:
(answer page)

God's gift to us...

How much _more_ shall your _heavenly_ father give the _Holy_ _Spirit_ to those who _ask_ him.

Luke 11:13

↓

Spirit gives →
Gifts
fruit
Offices

Gifts of the Spirit
- Wisdom
- Knowledge
- faith
- healing
- miracles
- prophecy
- distinguishing spirits
- tongues
- interpretation of tongues

Offices of the Spirit
1. apostles
2. prophets
3. evangelists
4. pastors
5. teachers

A comparison of fruit:

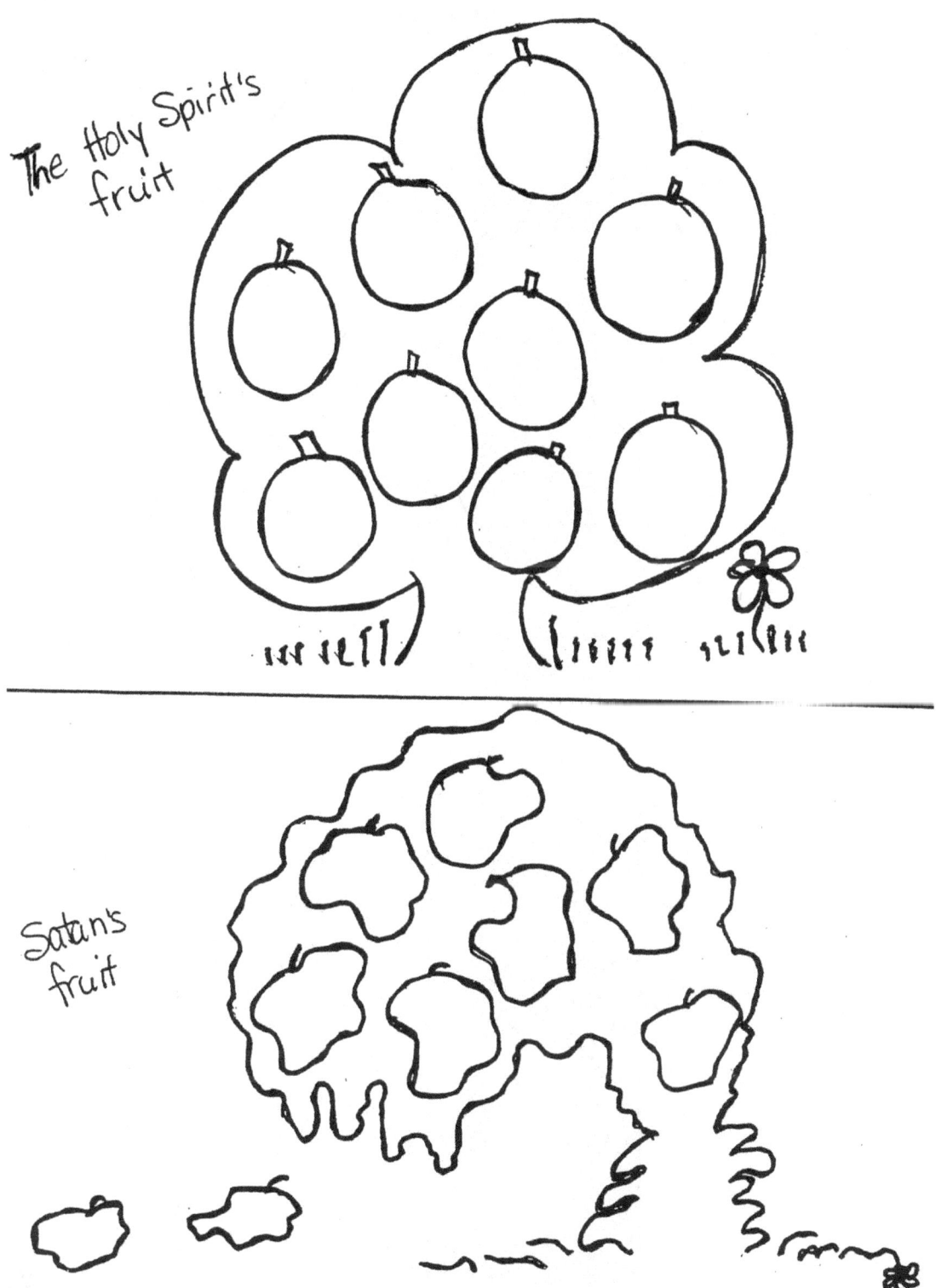

A comparison of fruit:
(answer page)

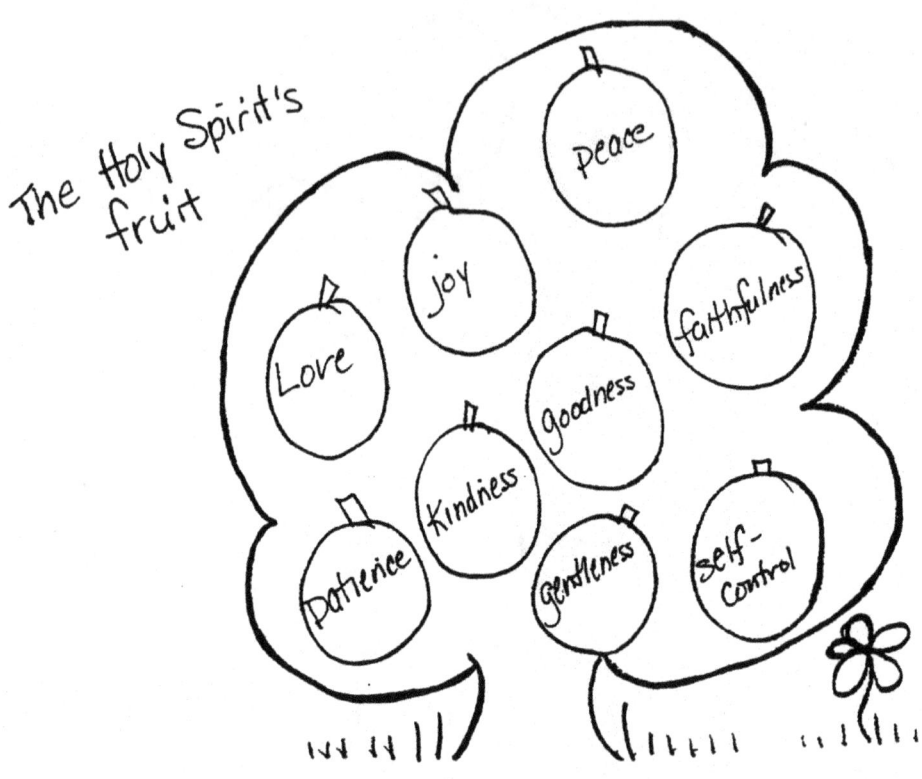

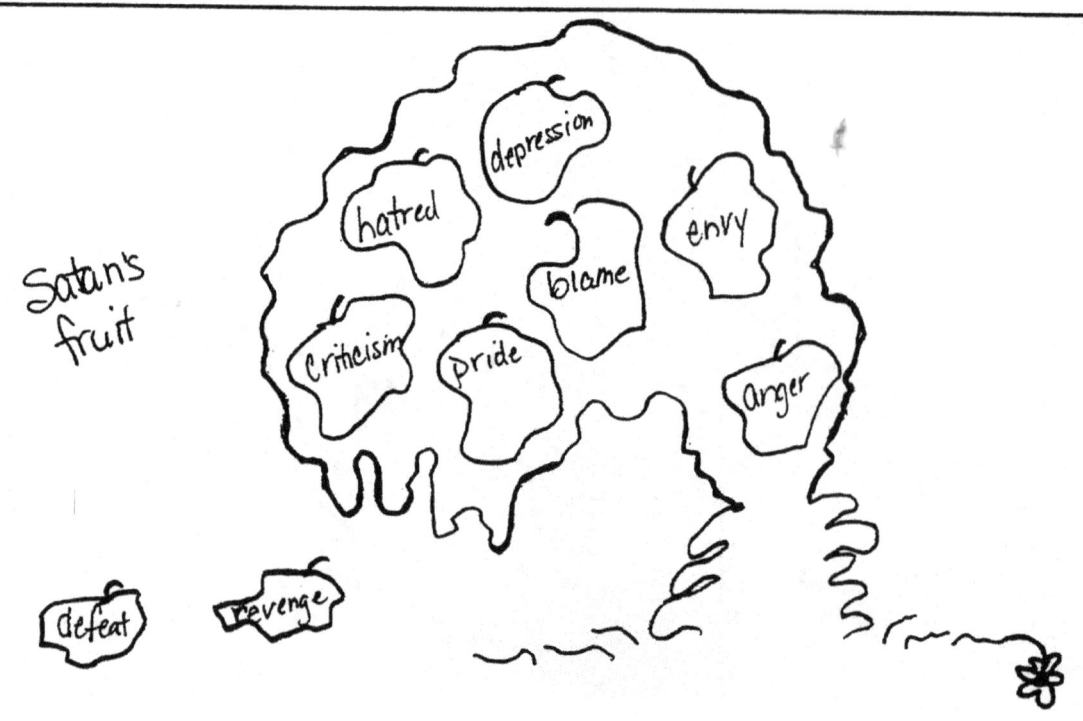

Lesson #10: **Two Christian sacraments: baptism and communion**

The 3 R's
R _____
R _____
R _____

① _____

This is my _____ , _____ for you.
This is the new _____ in my blood.

We'll eat it in heaven at the _____ of the _____

bread = _____

wine = _____

Do this in _____ of me
When you eat this, you do show forth the _____ _____ until He comes.

Make sure you have a _____ before you eat it or you could be _____ and _____ .
You receive _____ , new _____ with God each time you eat it.

② _____

water   holy spirit   fire

Do you confess Jesus as your _____ & _____ ? I baptise you in the name of the _____

Picture of died with _____ raised with _____

God delights in our public confession
If ___ confess ___ before ___
I'll confess ___ before my ___ !
Can you go to heaven without being baptised? _____

2 views:
1. baptised at _____
2. baptised after you've accepted _____ in your _____ ! _____ on the _____

(answer page)

The 3 R's — **re**member, **re**pent, **re**commit

Lesson #10: Two Christian sacraments: baptism and communion

① The Lord's Supper

This is my _body_, _broken_ for you.
This is the new _covenant_ in my blood.

We'll eat it in heaven at the marriage _Supper_ of the lamb.

bread = body

wine =

Do this in _remembrance_ of me
When you eat this, you do show forth the _Lord's_ _death_ until He comes.

Make sure you have a _clean_ _heart_ before you eat it or you could be _sick_ and _die_.
You receive _blessing_, new _closeness_ with God each time you eat it.

---

② Baptism

Water — _Washing_ _away_ _Sin_

holy spirit — _Power_

fire — _Suffering_

Do you confess Jesus as your Lord & Savior? I baptise you in the name of the _father_, _Son_, _holy spirit_

Witnesses

Picture of
died with _Christ_
raised with _Christ_

2 views:
1. baptised at _birth_
2. baptised after you've accepted _Jesus_ in your _heart_

God delights in our _public_ _confession_
If _you_ confess _me_ before _men_
I'll confess _you_ before my _Father_!
Can you go to heaven without being baptised? _Yes_! _thief_ on the _cross_

Lesson 11: The Ten Commandments

**command**

1. Thou shalt have no other _____ before me.

2. Thou shalt not make unto thee any _____ image.

3. Thou shalt not take the _____ of the Lord thy God in _____.

4. Remember the _____ day, to keep it _____.

5. Honor thy _____ and thy _____.

6. Thou shalt not _____.

7. Thou shalt not commit _____.

8. Thou shalt not _____.

9. Thou shalt not bear _____ witness against thy _____.

10. Thou shalt not _____.

Lesson 11:   The Ten Commandments *(answer page)*

 #   command

1. Thou shalt have no other *gods* before me.

2. Thou shalt not make unto thee any *graven* image.

3. Thou shalt not take the *name* of the Lord thy God in *vain*.

4. Remember the *Sabbath* day, to keep it *holy*.

5. Honor thy *father* and thy *mother*.

6. Thou shalt not *murder*.

7. Thou shalt not commit *adultery*.

8. Thou shalt not *steal*.

9. Thou shalt not bear *false* witness against thy *neighbor*.

10. Thou shalt not *covet*.

The 10 Commandments-- in number pictures

1 God is #1	2 image	3 name
4 Sabbath pews	5 father and mother	6 not kill
7 adult - tree	8 not steal	9 looking for false fault (magnifying glass)
10 not covet friends things like ball & bat	The first 4 Commandments deal with our relationship with GOD	The last 6 Commandments deal with our relationship with Others

YOU write the 10 Commandments
(remember them from the pictures!)

Lesson 12: The Lord's _____

(the prayer He taught us to pray)

1. Our _____ who art in _____,

    hallowed by thy _____.

2. Thy kingdom _____, Thy will be _____

    on _____ as it is in _____.

3. Give us this _____ our daily _____

4. And forgive _____ our debts,

    as _____ forgive our debtors. {_____ x _____}

5. And lead us _____ into temptation,

    but deliver us from _____.

6. For thine is the _____

    and the _____

    and the _____ forever.

    Amen.

Lesson 12: The Lord's *Prayer*
(the prayer He taught us to pray)

(answer page)

1. Our *Father* who art in *heaven*

    hallowed by thy *name*.

2. Thy kingdom *come*, Thy will be *done*

    on *earth* as it is in *heaven*.

3. Give us this *day* our daily *bread*

4. And forgive *us* our debts,

    as *we* forgive our debtors. {70 x 7}

5. And lead us *not* into temptation,

    but deliver us from *evil*.

6. For thine is the *kingdom*

    and the *power*

    and the *glory* forever.   Amen.

Prayer is like...

_____ Celestial furniture!

Operating a control panel in a quiet _____

making bombs go off in _____ away place that you can't _____

_____ the holes; put in the _____ ; string the electrical wire, _____ throws the switch

_____ lays the ax at the root of problem

_____ is the clean-up work

Prayer is _____ in _____.
Examining _____ in the presence of God.
I looked for a _____ to stand in the _____."
God may limit his activity sometimes, to move only when _____ _____.

d _____
d _____
d _____

There is no _____ in prayer! No human pride can live in true prayer.

Enemy Resistance
① drowsiness; overcome by _____
_____ changing _____ positions
reading Scripture out _____.
② restless activity; overcome by
_____ withdrawal
planning for a quiet _____
and a quiet _____

Extended time
Sometimes breakthrough after _____ hr.
No flitting like a _____
pray on one topic 'til you get released

No double-mindedness
Steadiness of _____ toward issue
Always _____ by Christ
Mueller prayed for _____ friends for _____ yrs

"There is no snare in prayer"   "No one struts before God"

Prayer is like...

moving Celestial furniture!	Operating a control panel in a quiet **place**	making bombs go off in <s>far</s> away places that you can't **see**
dig the holes; put in the **poles**; string the electrical wire → God **throws the switch**	**Prayer** lays the ax at the root of **problem**	**Service** is the clean-up work

Prayer is **Confiding** in **God**.
Examining **everything** in the presence of God.
"I looked for a **man** to stand in the **gap**"
God may limit his activity sometimes, to move only when **men pray**.

d **esire**
d **iscipline**
d **elight**

There is no **snare** in prayer! No human pride can live in true prayer.

Enemy Resistance
① drowsiness; overcome by **Singing** **Pacing** changing **body** positions reading Scripture **outloud**.
② restless activity: overcome by **world** withdrawal planning for a quiet **place** and a quiet **time**

Extended time
  Sometimes breakthrough after **2** hrs
No flitting like a **bird**
  pray on one topic 'til you get release.
No double-mindedness
  Steadiness of **mind** toward issue
  Always **rewarded &praised** by Christ
Mueller prayed for **5** friends for **20** yrs.

Lesson 13: Development of the concept of sacrificial atonement in biblical history:

> Without the shedding of _____ there is no remission of _____.
>
> sin / blood _____ covering _____ = _____

(1) Man's attempt to _____ his own guilt.
~_____~

God's _____: the skin of a _____. This required the shedding of _____.

God must have _____ them from the beginning what was an acceptable _____; _____ had to be _____.

(2) Cain offered ___ and _____.
~ man's own efforts~

Abel offered a _____.
~ _____ atonement~

(3) Job _____ for his sons every morning, in case they had sinned.

(4) Noah took ___ of every kind of animal into the ark--but ___ of every clean animal (Gen. 7:21, 8:20).

(5) The Levites offered

				, etc.
				_____ sacrifices
___	___	___	___	

(6) At the time of Christ's birth, the shepherds were guarding the sacrificial _____ that would be used in the worship at the _____.

(7) Now, "Behold the _____ of _____ who taketh away the _____ of the world." No further sacrifices are _____ -- _____.

Lesson 13: Development of the concept of sacrificial atonement in biblical history:
(answer page)

> Without the shedding of *blood* there is no remission of *sin*.
>
> *blood covers sin = forgiveness, just as* **Red** covering *red* = *white*

(1) Man's attempt to *cover* his own guilt. ~*fig leaves*~   God's *solution*: the skin of a *beast*. This required the shedding of *blood*.

God must have told them from the beginning what was an acceptable sacrifice; blood had to be shed.

(2) Cain offered *nuts* and *seeds*.  Abel offered a *lamb*.
~ man's own efforts~   ~ blood atonement~

(3) Job *sacrificed* for his sons every morning, in case they had sinned.

(4) Noah took *two* of every kind of animal into the ark--but *seven* of every clean animal (Gen. 7:21, 8:20).

(5) The Levites offered *(so long as there was a tabernacle/ temple)*

lambs	bulls	doves	pigeons	, etc. *continual* sacrifices

(6) At the time of Christ's birth, the shepherds were guarding the sacrificial *lambs* that would be used in the worship at the *temple*.

(7) Now, "Behold the *Lamb* of *God* who taketh away the *sins* of the world." No further sacrifices are *needed* -- *to accomplish salvation*.

Lesson 14: The Tabernacle

The furnishings of the Tabernacle make the shape of a cross: on the left tip is the menorah (Holy Spirit), on the right tip is the table of showbread (Yeshua/Jesus), top is Almighty God (mercy seat/ lid of atonement on the ark of the covenant). Where the two lines meet is the altar of incense (prayers of the saints/us). The Tabernacle is a picture of the three aspects of the Godhead, and of the Gospel.

Lesson 14: The Tabernacle *(answer page)*

Lesson 15: The Apostles' Creed

1. I believe in God the Father Almighty,
   2. maker of heaven and earth,

3. And in Jesus Christ His only son, our Lord,
   4. who was conceived by the Holy Spirit,
   5. born of the virgin Mary,
   6. suffered under Pontius Pilate,
   7. was crucified, dead, and buried;
   8. He descended into hell;
   9. the third day He arose from the dead;
   10. He ascended into heaven
   11. and sitteth at the right hand of God the Father Almighty;
   12. from thence He shall come to judge the quick and the dead.

13. I believe in the Holy Spirit,
    14. the holy catholic church,
    15. the communion of saints,
    16. the forgiveness of sins,
    17. the resurrection of the body,
    18. and the life everlasting.

Amen.

The Apostles' Creed *in pictures*

A-men

Lesson 16:   The Heidelberg Catechism

A group of serious Christians in Europe taught the Heidelberg Catechism to their children during World War II, to prepare them to find their hope in Christ if they were ever torn from their parents by the Nazis.

(see next page ☞)

Bible pledge of allegiance

I pledge allegiance to the Bible, God's holy word.

I'll make it a light unto my path
   and a lamp unto my feet.

I'll hide its words in my heart
   that I might not sin against Thee.

The Heidelberg Catechism*

Question:

"What is your only (1)_____ in (2)_____ and in (3)_____?"

Answer:

"That I belong--body and (4)_____, in life and in death--not to (5)_____ but to my faithful Savior (6)_____ (7)_____, who at the (8)_____ of His own (9)_____ has fully paid for all my (10)_____ and has completely (11)_____ me from the dominion of the (12)_____; that He protects me so well that without the (13)_____ of my Father in heaven not a (14)_____ can fall from my (15)_____; indeed, that (16)_____ must (17)_____ His purpose for (18)_____ salvation.

Therefore, by His (19)_____ (20)_____, He also assures me of eternal (21)_____, and makes me wholeheartedly (22)_____ and (23)_____ from now on to (24)_____ for (25)_____."

* Say this aloud with your teacher until you can fill in the blanks from your own memory! Then write the answers here.

The Heidelberg Catechism* *(answer page)*

Question:

"What is your only (1) *comfort* in (2) *life* and in (3) *death*?"

Answer:

"That I belong--body and (4) *soul*, in life and in death--not to (5) *myself* but to my faithful Savior (6) *Jesus* (7) *Christ*, who at the (8) *cost* of His own (9) *blood* has fully paid for all my (10) *sins* and has completely (11) *freed* me from the dominion of the (12) *devil*; that He protects me so well that without the (13) *will* of my Father in heaven not a (14) *hair* can fall from my (15) *head*; indeed, that (16) *everything* must (17) *fit* His purpose for (18) *my* salvation.

Therefore, by His (19) *Holy* (20) *Spirit*, He also assures me of eternal (21) *life*, and makes me wholeheartedly (22) *willing* and (23) *ready* from now on to (24) *live* for (25) *Him*."

* Say this aloud with your teacher until you can fill in the blanks from your own memory! Then write the answers here.

The Heidelberg Catechism *in pictures*

Lesson 17: Judgments

The pagan is judged according to _____.

The believer is judged according to the _____ of _____.

For the believer there will be _____ punishment, only _____.

Rewards

1. "I am coming soon, and my _____ is with me" (Rev. 22:12).

2. "_____ is your reward in _____" (Luke 6:23).

3. "He rewards those who earnestly _____ _____" (Hebrews 11:6).

4. "Each will receive his _____ reward, according to his own _____" (1 Corinthians 3:8).

5. "And the Lord will _____ each man for his righteousness and his faithfulness" (1 Sam. 26:23).

6. "Know that whatever _____ thing each one _____, this he will receive _____ from the _____" (Ephesians 6:8).

7. "For the Son of Man is going to _____ in the glory of His _____ with His angels, and will _____ every man according to his _____" (Matt. 16:27).

"...his work will be shown for what it is, because the Day will bring it to light. It will be revealed with fire, and the fire will test the quality of each man's work. If what he has built survives, he will receive his reward. If it is burned up, he will suffer loss; he himself will be saved, but only as one escaping through the flames" *(1 Corinthians 3:13-15).*

Lesson 17: *(answer page)*
Judgments

The pagan is judged according to *sin*.

The believer is judged according to the *holiness* of *Christ*.

For the believer there will be *no* punishment, only *rewards*.

Rewards

1. "I am coming soon, and my *reward* is with me" (Rev. 22:12).

2. "*Great* is your reward in *heaven*" (Luke 6:23).

3. "He rewards those who earnestly *seek Him*" (Hebrews 11:6).

4. "Each will receive his *own* reward, according to his own *labor*" (1 Corinthians 3:8).

5. "And the Lord will *repay* each man for his righteousness and his faithfulness" (1 Samuel 26:23).

6. "Know that whatever *good* thing each one *does*, this he will receive *back* from the *Lord*" (Ephesians 6:8).

7. "For the Son of Man is going to *come* in the glory of His *Father* with His angels, and will *repay* every man according to his *deeds*" (Matthew 16:27).

"...his work will be shown for what it is, because the Day will bring it to light. It will be revealed with fire, and the fire will test the quality of each man's work. If what he has built survives, he will receive his reward. If it is burned up, he will suffer loss; he himself will be saved, but only as one escaping through the flames" *(1 Corinthians 3:13-15).*

Crowns

Rev. 2:10: "And I will give you the (1)_____ of life."

1 Peter 5:4: "You will receive the (2)_____ crown of (3)_____."

2 Tim. 4:8: "...laid up for (4)___ the crown of righteousness...to all who have (5)_____ His (6)_____."

Rev. 4:4: "...and (7)_____ crowns were on their (8)_____."

Rev. 4:10: "...and will (9)_____ their crowns before the (10)_____."

Crowns *(answer page)*

Rev. 2:10: And I will give you the (1) *crown* of life.

1 Peter 5:4: You will receive the (2) *unfading* crown of (3) *glory*.

2 Tim. 4:8: ...laid up for (4) *me* the crown of righteousness...to all who have (5) *loved* His (6) *appearing*.

Rev. 4:4: ...and (7) *golden* crowns were on their (8) *heads*.

Rev. 4:10: ...and will (9) *cast* their crowns before the (10) *throne*.

Answers:

1. crown	2. unfading	3. glory	4. me	5. love
6. appearing	7. golden	8. heads	9. cast	10. throne

Practicing overcoming: Lesson 18: The enemy

Angels / Lucifer (choir director of ___ ____)	**Pride/ Sin:** Isaiah 14:13 (1) ___ _____ ascend to heaven. (2) ___ _____ raise my throne above the stars of heaven. (3) ___ _____ sit on the mount of assembly. (4) ___ _____ ascend above the heights of the clouds. (5) ___ _____ make myself like the Most High.
Transferred authority:	1/3 were cast down
(1) "He [Christ] disarmed the _____ and authorities. He made a _____ display of them, having triumphed _____ then through Him" (Col. 2:15).	Rev. 12:9: "Satan has been thrown _____, and _____ with him."
(2) God gave authority to _____. "All authority has been given to ___, in heaven and on _____" (Matthew 28:18).	Fallen angels were renamed _____.
(3) _____ gave authority to ___. "They overcame him by the _____ of the Lamb and the _____ of their testimony" (Rev. 12:11).	Lucifer was renamed the _____, and was made _____ of the _____ of the air.
(4) **Messiah** came that we might have abundant _____.	The **devil** creates _____ _____; he lies and tempts; he counterfeits; he steals, _____, and destroys.

Practicing overcoming: Lesson 18: The enemy

(answer page)

Angels: **Head** Angels — Michael (warriors), Gabriel (messengers), Lucifer (choir director of high praises; head of worship), God	**Pride/ Sin:** Isaiah 14:13 (1) *I will* ascend to heaven. (2) *I will* raise my throne above the stars of heaven. (3) *I will* sit on the mount of assembly. (4) *I will* ascend above the heights of the clouds. (5) *I will* make myself like the Most High.
Transferred authority:	1/3 were cast down
(1) "He [Christ] disarmed the *rulers* and authorities. He made a *public* display of them, having triumphed *over* them through Him" (Col. 2:15).	Rev. 12:9: "Satan has been thrown *down* and *angels* with him."
(2) God gave authority to *Christ*. "All authority has been given to *me*, in heaven and on *earth*" (Matthew 28:18).	Fallen angels were renamed *demons*.
(3) *Christ* gave authority to *us*. "They overcame him by the *blood* of the Lamb and the *word* of their testimony" (Rev. 12:11).	Lucifer was renamed the *devil*, and was made *prince* of the *power* of the air.
(4) **Messiah** came that we might have abundant *life*.	The **devil** creates *demonic music*; he lies and tempts; he counterfeits; he steals, *kills*, and destroys.

Lesson 19: The believer's armor

"…having done everything, ____ _____" (Ephesians 6:13).

Note that we have no armor on the back of us! So, never _____.

Keep on putting it on:
1. Helmet of _____.
2. Shield of _____.
3. Breastplate of _____.
4. Sword of the _____.
5. Belt of _____.
6. Feet shod with the gospel of _____.

"…draw near to _____; resist the _____ and he will _____ from you" (James 4:7)

Fight with the words of your mouth:
1. _____
2. _____
3. _____
confessions.

orders:
①
② be on alert
③

Human _____ can be caused by the _____'s _____ in _____ unseen places.

The _____ of _____:
"For our _____ is not [only] against _____ and _____, but against the _____, against the _____, against the world _____ of this _____, against the spiritual forces of _____ in the heavenly places" (Ephesians. 6:12).

Lesson 19: The believer's armor *(answer page)*

"...having done everything, *stand firm*" (Ephesians 6:13).
Note that we have no armor on the back of us! So, never *flee*.

Fight with the words of your mouth:
1. Praise
2. Promises
3. Positive confessions.

orders:
1. Pray
2. be on alert
3. Persevere

Keep on putting it on:
1. Helmet of *salvation*.
2. Shield of *faith*.
3. Breastplate of *righteousness*.
4. Sword of the *Spirit*.
5. Belt of *truth*.

Feet shod with the gospel of *peace*.

"...draw near to *God*;
resist the *devil* and he will *flee*
from you" (James 4:7)

Human *conflict* can be caused by the *devil's schemes* in unseen places.

The *gospel* of *peace*:

"For our *struggle* is not [only] against *flesh* and *blood*, but against the *rulers*, against the *powers*, against the world *forces* of this *darkness*, against the spiritual forces of *wickedness* in the heavenly places" (Ephesians 6:12).

Verses for spiritual warfare

WEAKNESS

Phil. 4:14: "I can do _____ things through _____ Who strengthens _____."

1 Corinthians 15:57: "Thanks be to _____, Who _____ leads me in triumph."

FEAR

Psalm 23: "Though I _____ through the _____ of the shadow of _____, I will _____ _____ _____.

Psalm 4:8: "In peace I will both _____ down and _____, for thou alone, oh Lord, dost _____ me to _____ in _____."

HEALING

Psalm 91:10: "No _____ will _____ you, nor will any _____ come near your _____."

Psalm 103:2-3: "Forget none of His benefits, Who pardons all your _____, Who _____ all your _____."

Verses for spiritual warfare *(answer page)*

WEAKNESS

Phil. 4:14: "I can do *all* things through *Christ* Who strengthens me."

1 Corinthians 15:57: "Thanks be *to God*, Who *always* leads me in triumph."

FEAR

Psalm 23: "Though I *walk* through the *valley* of the shadow of *death*, I will *fear* no *evil*.

Psalm 4:8: "In peace I will both *lie* down and *sleep*, for thou alone, oh Lord, dost *make* me to *dwell* in *safety*."

HEALING

Psalm 91:10: "No *evil* will *befall* you, nor will any *plague* come near your *dwelling*."

Psalm 103:2-3: "Forget none of His benefits, Who pardons all your *iniquities*, Who heals all your *diseases*."

More spiritual warfare verses

LOVE OF GOD MORE THAN PEOPLE

1 Samuel 2:20: "They that _____ Me, I will _____."

MEANING OF LIFE. WHAT AM I DOING ON EARTH?

Jeremiah 29:11: "For I know the _____ that I have for _____; plans for _____ and not for _____; to give _____ a _____ and a _____."

ANXIETY AND WORRY

Philippians 4:6-7: "Have no _____ about _____, but in everything, by prayer and supplication…with thanksgiving…let your request be made known to _____, and the _____ of _____ will guard your hearts and your minds in Christ Jesus."

LACK OF MONEY

Philippians 4:19: "My God shall _____ _____ my _____, according to His _____ in glory, by Christ Jesus."

More spiritual warfare verses *(answer page)*

LOVE OF GOD MORE THAN PEOPLE

1 Samuel 2:20: "They that *honor* Me, I will *honor*."

MEANING OF LIFE. WHAT AM I DOING ON EARTH?

Jeremiah 29:11: "For I know the *plans* that I have for *you*; plans for *welfare* and not for *calamity*; to give *you* a *future* and a *hope*."

ANXIETY AND WORRY

Philippians 4:6-7: "Have no *anxiety* about *anything*, but in everything, by prayer and supplication…with thanksgiving…let your request be made known to *God*, and the peace of *God* will guard your hearts and your minds in Christ Jesus."

LACK OF MONEY

Philippians. 4:19: "My God shall *supply all* my *need*, according to His *riches* in glory, by Christ Jesus."

Alphabet verses

A = **A**ll have sinned and come short of the glory of God. (Romans 3:23)

B = **B**elieve on the Lord Jesus Christ, and thou shalt be saved. (Acts 16:31)

C = **C**hildren, obey your parents in the Lord, for this is right. (Ephesians 6:1)

D = **D**epart from evil and do good. (Psalm 34:14)

E = **E**ven a child is known by his doings. (Proverbs 20:11)

F = **F**ear not, for I am with thee. (Isaiah 43:5)

G = **G**od is love. (1 John 4:8)

H = **H**onor thy Father and thy mother. (Exodus 20:12)

I = "**I**f ye shall ask anything in my name, I will do it." (John 14:14)

J = **J**esus saith unto him, "I am the way, the truth, and the life. No man cometh unto the Father, but by Me." (John 14:6)

K = **K**eep thy tongue from evil. (Psalm 34:13)

L = **L**ook unto me, and be ye saved. (Isaiah 45:22)

M = **M**y son, give me thine heart. (Proverbs 23:26)

N = **N**o man can serve two masters. (Matthew 6:24)

O = **O** give thanks unto the Lord, for He is good. (Psalm 118:1)

P = **P**raise ye the Lord for it is good to sing praises unto our God. (Psalm 147:1)

Q = **Q**uit you like men, be strong. (1 Corinthians 16:13)

R = **R**emember the Sabbath day, to keep it holy. (Exodus 20:8)

S = **S**eek ye the Lord while He may be found. (Isaiah 55:6)

T = **T**hou God seest me. (Genesis 16:13)

U = **U**nto Thee, O god, do we give thanks. (Psalm 75:1)

V = **V**erily, verily I say unto you, whatsoever ye shall ask the Father in my name, He will give it you. (John 16:23)

W = **W**hen I am afraid, I will trust in Thee. (Psalm 56:3)

X = E**x**ceeding great and precious promises are given unto us. (2 Peter 1:4)

Y = "**Y**e are the light of the world." (Matthew 5:14)

Z = **Z**ion heard and was glad. (Psalm 97:8)

Lesson 20: How to overcome temptation

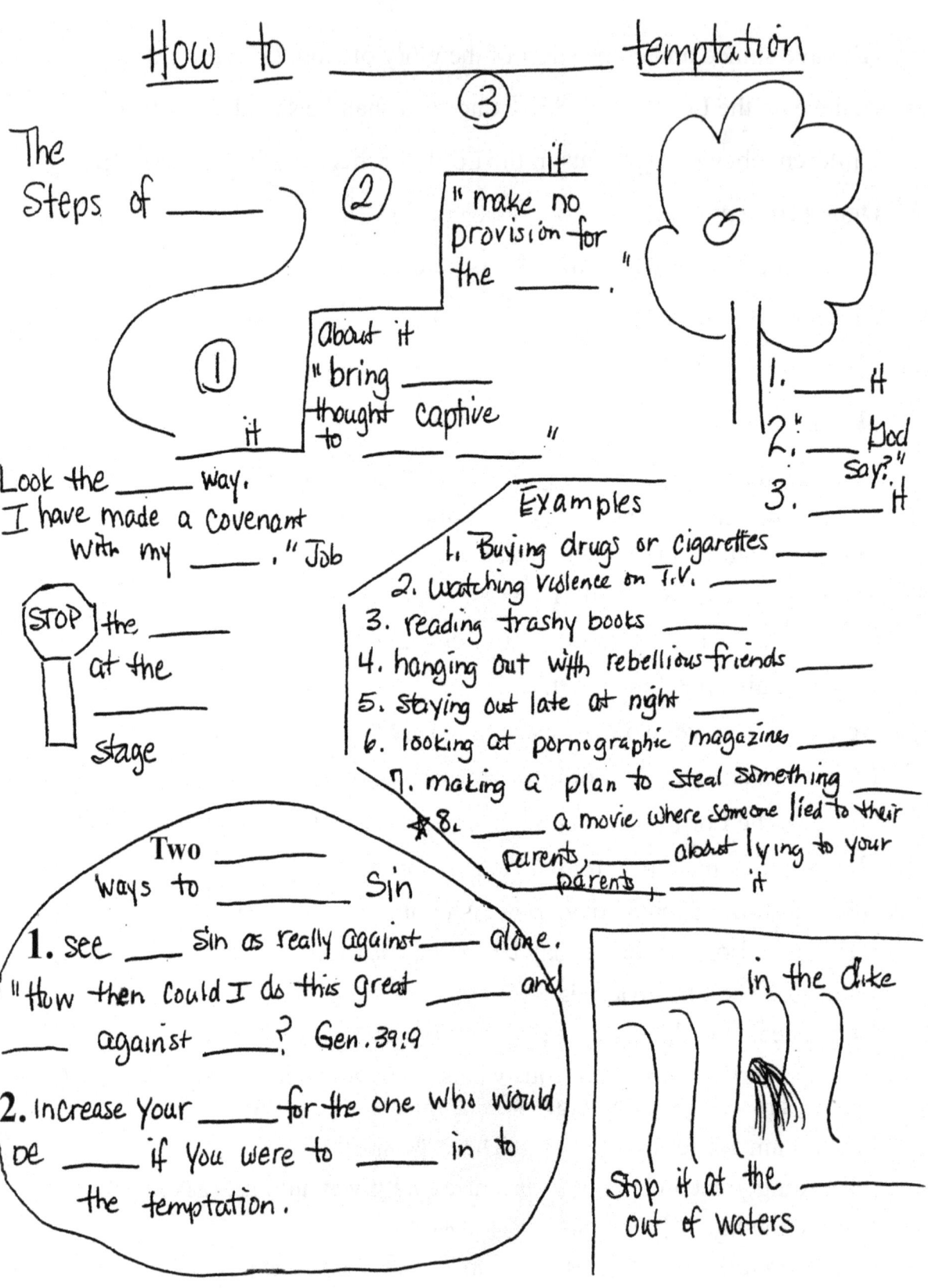

Lesson 20: How to overcome temptation *(answer page)*

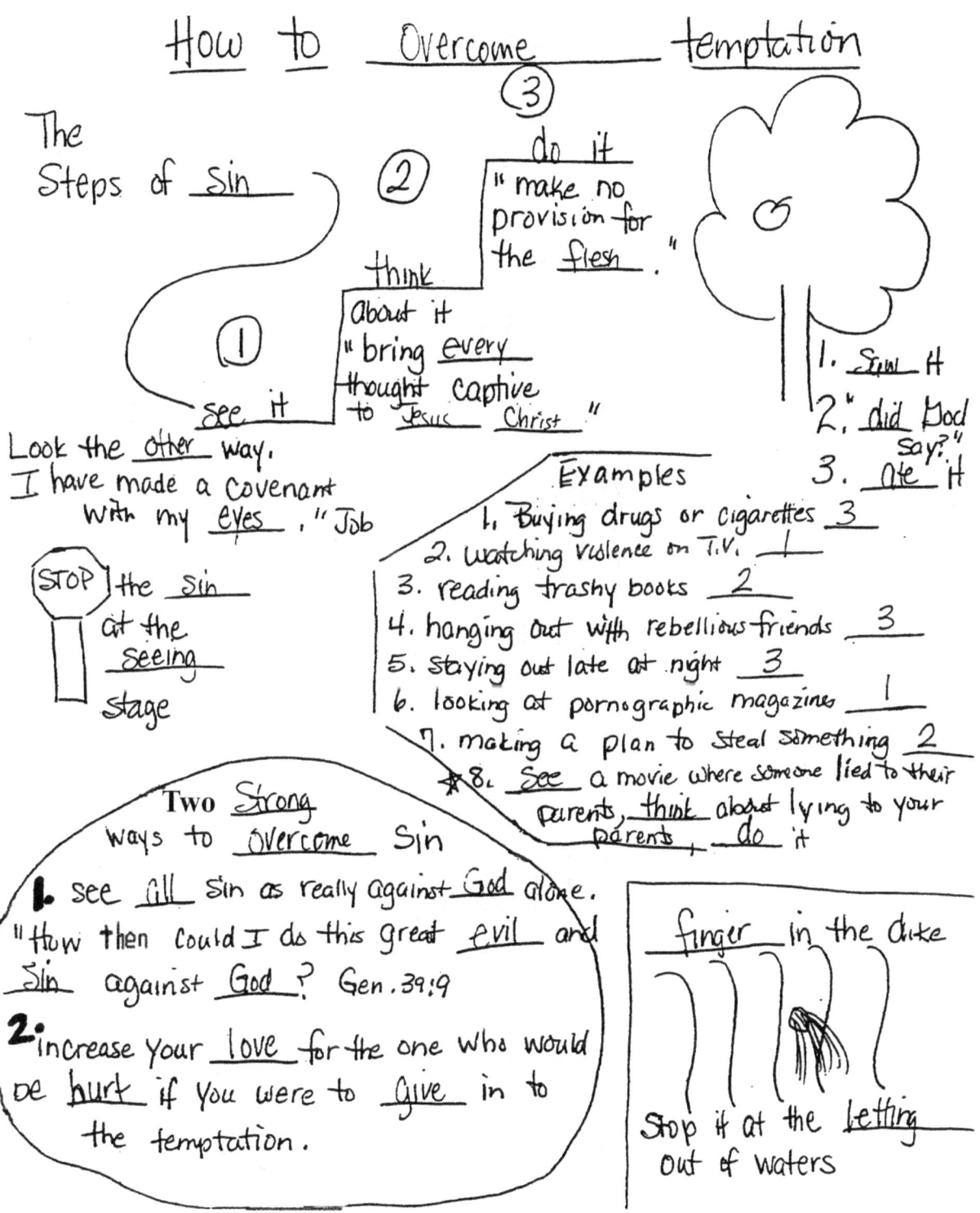

The Cross (the Stake)

"I have been crucified with Christ" (Galatians 2:20).

The dominion of sin is *broken*.

Through Christ, we *do* have the power to resist temptation.

Lesson 21: Choosing wise companions

Choose _____ Companions

How to spot a _____ Companion

Look for someone...
- Who puts _____ first
- Who has moral character in all his _____
- Who influences _____ to be closer to _____.

- May _____ _____ like a clown at all.
- May look _____ on the outside but watch the _____ decisions he makes _____ and _____
- A rebellious person is a _____
- An angry person is a _____

You may help a fool
1. You don't confide in _____
2. _____ stay in control of the environment and have a _____ of escape.

VERSES

1. I never _____ in the company of revelers (_____ people) Jer. 15:17
2. _____ Companions corrupt _____ character. (_____ __:__)
3. But a companion of _____ suffers _____. Proverbs 13:20
4. Do not _____ in the way of _____ nor _____ in the seat of scoffers. Psalm 1
5. A companion of gluttons disgraces his _____. Proverbs 28:7

Caution !
* Lots of time spent with a _____ friend will result in you being _____ astray _____ and having great _____ _____.

Lesson 21: Choosing wise companions *(answer page)*

Choose **Wise** Companions

How to spot a *Wise Companion* / *fool*

Wise Companion:
Look for someone...
- who puts **God** first
- who has moral character in all his **actions**
- who influences **you** to be closer to **God**.

Fool:
- May **not** **look** like a clown at all.
- May look **fine** on the outside but watch the **poor** decisions he makes **over** and **over**
- A rebellious person is a **fool**
- An angry person is a **fool**

You may help a fool *If*
1. You don't confide in **him**
2. **You** stay in control of the environment and have a **way** of escape.

VERSES

1. I never **sat** in the company of revelers (**party** people) Jer. 15:17
2. **Bad** companions corrupt **good** character. (_____:__)
3. But a companion of **fools** suffers **harm**. Proverbs 13:20
4. Do not **stand** in the way of **sinners** nor **sit** in the seat of scoffers. Psalm 1
5. A companion of gluttons disgraces his **father**. Proverbs 28:7

Caution!
★ Lots of time spent with a **bad** friend will result in you being **led** astray **now** and having great **sorrow** **later**.

Lesson 22: How love acts: 1 Corinthians 13

Lesson 22: How love acts: 1 Corinthians 13 *(answer page)*

Lesson 23: We lack nothing

The Lord is my shepherd (Psalm 23)

The _____ ___ my _____, I shall not _____.

He makes me to ___ _____ in _____ pastures.

He _____ me beside _____ _____.

He _____ my soul.

He leads me in the _____ of righteousness for His _____ _____.

Yeah, though I _____ through the _____ of the shadow of _____

I will fear no _____, for thou art _____ _____.

Thy _____ and thy _____ they _____ me.

Thou preparest a _____ before me in the presence of my _____.

Thou anointest my _____ with _____.

My _____ runneth _____.

Surely _____ and _____ shall _____ me all the days of my _____,

And I shall _____ in the _____ of the Lord _____.

_____ ___

81

Lesson 23: We lack nothing (answer page)

The Lord is my shepherd (Psalm 23)

The *Lord* is my shepherd, I shall not *want*.

He makes me to *lie down* in *green* pastures.

He *leads* me beside *still* waters.

He *restores* my *soul*.

He leads me in the *paths* of righteousness for His *name's sake*.

Yeah, though I *walk* through the *valley* of the shadow of *death*,

I will fear no *evil*, for Thou art *with me*.

They *rod* and Thy *staff*, they *comfort* me.

Thou preparest a *table* before me in the presence of my *enemies*.

Thou anointest my *head* with *oil*.

My *cup* runneth *over*.

Surely *goodness* and *mercy* shall *follow* me all the days of my *life*.

And I shall *dwell* in the *house* of the Lord *forever*.

Psalm 23

The Lord is my shepherd – in pictures

Can you say the whole psalm by just looking at these pictures?

The Lord is My Shepherd– in a round, to sing

The Lord is my shepherd

I'll walk with Him always.

He leads me by still waters

I'll walk with Him always.

Chorus:

Always, always, I'll walk with Him always

Always, always, I'll walk with Him always.

Lesson 24: Obedience

What happens…

…when you disobey _____? : _____

…when you don't follow a _____? : _____

…when you mess up on a _____ _____? : _____

$2 + 2 = 5$ ← wrong answer

☐ - 3 = ☐

☐ - 1 = ☐ ← wrong conclusion

Keys to obedience:

--1-- _____. (listen to the Ethel Barrett Bible story of young Samuel at Eli's temple)

_____ obedience is ____ _____.

--2-- _____.

_____ is important to _____.

Sarah obeyed Abraham, calling him _____.

--3-- _____. (sing the hymn, *Trust and Obey*)

Godly obedience is _____ -- not asking _____ first.

If we get into the _____ of obedience to our _____,

_____, and godly _____, we will learn to

always be saying, "_____" to _____.

--4— Obedience is _____ than doing something else that you _____

the other person will like more. If your Dad asks you to clean the

_____ but instead you bring him your _____, he won't be

_____. "To _____ is _____ than

_____" (1 Samuel 15:22).

Lesson 24: Obedience
(answer page)

What happens…

…when you disobey *instructions*? **Trouble.**

…when you don't follow a *recipe*? **Failure.**

…when you mess up on a *math problem*? **Trouble.**

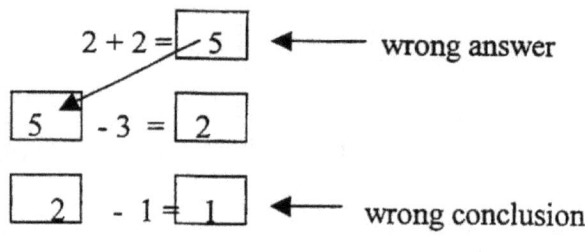

Keys to obedience:

--1—***Instant***. (listen to the Ethel Barrett Bible story of young Samuel at Eli's temple)

Delayed obedience is **no good**.

--2—***Joyful***.

Attitude is important to **God**.

Sarah obeyed Abraham, calling him ***lord***.

--3—***Habitual***. (sing the hymn, *Trust and Obey*)

Godly obedience is ***unquestioning*** -- not asking ***Why?*** first.

If we get into the ***habit*** of obedience to our ***parents, grandparents,*** and godly ***teachers***, we will learn to always be saying, "***Yes***" to ***Christ***.

--4—Obedience is ***better*** than doing something else that you ***think*** the other person will like more. If your Dad asks you to clean the ***garage*** but instead you bring him your ***hamburger*** he won't be ***pleased***. "To ***obey*** is ***better*** than ***sacrifice*** (1 Samuel 15:22).

Obedience and disobedience: A comparison of results

1. Obedience brings _____.
   Disobedience brings _____.

2. Obedience will lead you into _____ and into knowing godly things that are _____ from other people. "We have _____ and then have come to _____" (John 6:69).

3. We can learn obedience by _____ example or by verbal _____ , OR by the experience of _____ knocks.

Biblical examples of disobedience:

1. Lot's _____ disobeyed by looking _____, and was turned into a pillar of _____.

2. Moses _____ the rock instead of _____ to it, and was not allowed to _____ into the promised land.

3. Because the children of Israel disobeyed, it took them _____ years to travel a distance that should have been an _____-day journey.

4. Solomon had _____ wives, princesses, and _____ concubines, and his wives turned his heart _____ from God (1 Kings 11:3-4).

5. "You have eaten from the tree about which I commanded you saying 'You shall _____ eat from it.' _____ is the ground because of you" (Gen. 3:17).

6. "The people sat down to _____ and _____" and rose up to _____.
   They have quickly turned _____ from the way which I commanded them. They have made a molten _____ and worshiped it .... God said, 'Now let Me alone, that I may _____ them" (Ex. 32:6-8).

7. "But _____ rose up to _____ from the presence of the LORD ....
   And the LORD appointed a great _____ to _____ Jonah" (Jonah 1:3,17)

8. Saul disobeyed and offered a burnt offering -- which was the priest's job alone (1 Sam. 13). "You have acted _____ and have _____ kept the command of the _____. Now your kingdom shall ____ endure."

Lesson: Whenever I am tempted to disobey, I shall _____ ask the LORD to help me to obey.

87

Obedience and disobedience: A comparison of results
(answer page)

1. Obedience brings *blessing*.
   Disobedience brings *trouble*.

2. Obedience will lead you into *wisdom* and into knowing godly things that are *hidden* from other people. "We have *believed (obeyed)* and then have come to *know* (John 6:69).

3. We can learn obedience by *written* example or by verbal *warning*, OR by the experience of *hard* knocks.

Biblical examples of disobedience:

1. Lot's *wife* disobeyed by looking *back*, and was turned into a pillar of *salt*.

2. Moses *struck* the rock instead of *speaking* to it, and was not allowed to *enter* into the promised land.

3. Because the children of Israel disobeyed, it took them *40* years to travel a distance that should have been an *11*-day journey.

4. Solomon had *700* wives, princesses, and *300* concubines, and his wives turned his heart *away* from God (1 Kings 11:3-4).

5. "You have eaten from the tree about which I commanded you saying 'You shall *not* eat from it.' *Cursed* is the ground because of you" (Gen. 3:17).

6. "The people sat down to *eat* and *drink*, and rose up to *play*.
   They have quickly turned *aside* from the way which I commanded them. They have made a molten *calf* and worshiped it .... God said, 'Now let Me alone, that I may *destroy* them" (Ex. 32:6-8).

7. "But *Jonah* rose up to *flee* from the presence of the LORD ....
   And the LORD appointed a great *fish* to *swallow* Jonah" (Jonah 1:3,17)

8. Saul disobeyed and offered a burnt offering -- which was the priest's job alone (1 Sam. 13). "You have acted *foolishly* and have *not* kept the command of the *Lord*. Now your kingdom shall *not* endure."

Lesson: Whenever I am tempted to disobey, I shall *quickly* ask the LORD to help me to obey.

Lesson 25: Faith vs. good works

How to get into heaven

If the proverbial St. Peter were to meet someone at the pearly gates and ask, "Why should I let you into my heaven?" some would give one of the following answers...

1. because I was _____.
2. because I was _____. } _____ answers!
3. because I never _____.

The _____ makes people _____ that they can get into _____ with these _____ _____.

Problems with good works

1. How _____ good works are _____?

2. What if you do a good work, but your _____ is wrong?
   "I'll water his yard, so he'll give me some apples."
   "I'll do good deeds to make you like me."
   "I'll take you for a ride on my bicycle so my sister can steal your money while you're gone."

3. What if you do good deeds for only a _____, then you do a _____ deed? Then you do good deeds, then bad deeds, and then you _____ in the middle of doing a _____ deed?

4. What if you are _____ to _____ but are _____ towards God? (or, vice versa)

5. What if your _____ are _____ but your outside deeds look _____?

6. What if you are _____ _____ but you _____ about it?

Lesson 25: Faith vs. good works   *(answer page)*

How to get into heaven

If the proverbial St. Peter were to meet someone at the pearly gates and ask, "Why should I let you into my heaven?" some would give one of the following answers...

1. because I was *good*.
2. because I was *loving*.
3. because I never *hurt anyone*.

Wrong answers!

The *devil* makes people *think* that they can get into *heaven* with these *good works*.

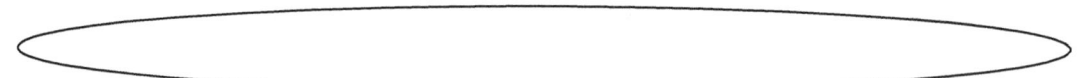

Problems with good works

1. How *many* good works are *enough* ?

2. What if you do a good work, but your *motive* is wrong?
   "I'll water his yard, so he'll give me some apples."
   "I'll do good deeds to make you like me."
   "I'll take you for a ride on my bicycle so my sister can steal your money while you're gone."

3. What if you do good deeds for only a *while*, then you do a *bad* deed? Then you do good deeds, then bad deeds, and then you *die* in the middle of doing a *bad* deed?

4. What if you are *kind* to *people* but are *angry* towards God? (or, vice versa)

5. What if your *thoughts* are *awful* but your outside deeds look *great* ?

6. What if you are *generous* but you *boast* about it?

Christ's good works

1. The Messiah was not just _____ ; He was _____. His works were _____ .

2. His good deed of redemption happened _____ , and will last for _____ . It is _____ . "It is _____ ."

3. His good deed was totally sacrificial. He had no ____ _____ .

   If we want to get into heaven on the basis of the Messiah's good work, what do we have to do? _____ (which means, _____).

   If we _____ , God will _____ us _____ !

Verses about being saved

1. "He _____ us, not on the basis of _____ which ____ have done...but according to _____ mercy" (Titus 3:5).

2. "For by _____ you have been saved, through _____ , and that not of _____ . It is the _____ of God, not as the result of _____ , that no one should _____ " (Eph. 2:9).

   If God _____ it, I _____ it, and that _____ it!

Doubt

_____ is from the _____ . He sends out _____ _____ (bad news) about God every day. He wants you to think that everything is impossible. _____ the devil by believing _____ ! You can (in some cases) doubt _____ , but never doubt _____ .

"God is not a _____ , that He should _____ ,
Nor a son of _____ , that He should change His _____ .
Has He not _____ and will He not _____ ?
Has He not _____ and will He not _____ ?" (Num. 23: 19)

Christ's good works   *(answer page)*

1. The Messiah was not just *good* ; He was *holy.* His works were *perfect* .

2. His good deed of redemption happened *once* , and will last for *all time* . It is *enough* . "It is *finished* ."

3. His good deed was totally sacrificial. He had no *bad motives* .

4. If we want to get into heaven on the basis of the Messiah's good work, what do we have to do? *Believe* (which means, *obey*).
If we *believe* , God will *make* us *good* !

Verses about being saved

1. "He *saved* us, not on the basis of *works* which *we* have done...but according to *His* mercy" (Titus 3:5).

2. "For by *grace* you have been saved, through *faith*, and that not of *yourselves* . It is the *gift* of God, not as the result of *works*, that no one should *boast* " (Eph. 2:9).

If God ***said*** *it, I* ***believe*** *it, and that* ***settles*** *it!*

Doubt

Doubt is from the *devil* . He sends out *bad press* (bad news) about God every day. He wants you to think that everything is impossible. *Fight* the devil by believing *God* ! You can (in some cases) doubt *people* , but never doubt *God* .

"God is not a *man* , that He should *lie* ,
Nor a son of *man* , that He should change His *mind* .
Has He not *spoken* and will He not *act* ?
Has He not *promised* and will He not *fulfill* ?" (Num. 23: 19)

Final section: Grasping the Bible

Children can gulp the Word

(synopsis of article by Renée Ellison; available in full in printed and ebook formats from www.homeschoolhowtos.com)

Let the word of Christ dwell in you RICHLY, the Bible says.

We can study five ways to get the Bible to take up residence in our children.

1. Irrigate the mind with a steady wash of scripture **by reading it from cover to cover, over and over**.

2. Take a look that is "up close and personal" ...**by memorizing specific verses**.

3. **Study the doctrine**, to gain a systematic thorough knowledge of the tenets of our faith and to help ground us against impostor religions.

4. **Train the character** through the frequent use of applicable scriptures.

5. **Train in hymnology**.

Goals for learning the books of the Bible

Mentally

1. To **take the fear out of using the Bible**...

    ...that it's too huge--too many pages and sections

    ...that it's a book for adults only

    ...that it's too complicated, conceptually.

2. To **master the sequence of main events, people and themes** so thoroughly that the student will be able to teach it to others. Anchored through the use of hand motions.

3. To **master the names of the books**--in order, by memory.

4. To be able to **find any verse** in the Bible within a few seconds,

    (a) naming which quarter of the Bible it is found in and

    (b) remembering the name of the book that precedes it and the name of the book that follows it.

Emotionally

That students will have a **confidence** in handling scripture for the rest of their lives--and will enjoy the fact that they really can understand it.

Spiritually

That students will come to **cherish scripture** because it brings them nearer to the Heavenly Father.

Lesson 26: The Bible: The inspired Book

How many books are in the Bible? _____
    in the Old Testament? _____
    in the New Testament? _____

How many years did it take to write it? _____
    on how many continents was it written? _____
    in how many languages was it first written? _____
    how many authors does it have? _____

At different _____, in different _____;
    each author's _____ story made one _____ _____ story.
The Bible is the only book that tells things _____ they happen
    and they ALL _____ _____.
God's Word can never be _____.
_____ and _____ may pass away, but His
    _____ will stand forever. (Matthew 24:35)

More copies of the _____ have been published than of any other
    book ever written; thousands of Bibles a day.
What is the farthest place the Bible has gone? _____ _____.

"All scripture is inspired by God and profitable for
        (1)_____, for
        (2)_____, for
        (3)_____, and for
        (4)_____ _____
        _____" (2 Timothy 3:16).
Read scripture as a _____ rather than as an _____.
_____ scripture, _____ scripture, _____ scripture, _____
    scripture. Use scripture as a jumping off point for you to _____
    _____.

Lesson 26: The Bible: The inspired book   *(answer page)*

How many books are in the Bible?   *66*
    in the Old Testament?   *39*
    in the New Testament?   *27*

How many years did it take to write it?   *1,600*
    on how many continents was it written?   *3* (Asia, Africa, Europe)
    in how many languages was it first written?   *3* (Hebrew, Aramaic, Greek)
    how many authors does it have?   *40*

At different *times*, in different *places*;
    each author's *small* story made one *big perfect* story.
The Bible is the only book that tells things *before* they happen and they ALL *come true*.
God's Word can never be *destroyed*.
Heaven and *earth* may pass away, but His *Word* will stand forever.
    (Matthew 24:35)

More copies of the *Bible* have been published than of any other book ever written; thousands of Bibles a day.
What is the farthest place the Bible has gone?   *the moon*.

"All scripture is inspired by God and profitable for
    (1)   *teaching*, for (2) *reproof*, for (3) *correction*, and for (4) *training in righteousness*" (2 Timothy 3:16).

Read scripture as a *devotee* rather than as an *intellectual*.
Think scripture, *speak* scripture, *pray* scripture, *do* scripture. Use scripture as a jumping off point for you to *love God*.

Lesson 27: Bible history one-minute survey: Key words and hand motions*

1. CREATION--hands in big circle
2. FALL--hands collapse
3. FLOOD--hands bubble up
4. NATIONS--fingers & arms shoot out
5. ABRAHAM--fist
6. ISAAC--2nd fist under 1st fist
7. JACOB--1st fist moved under Isaac's fist
8. JOSEPH--hold lapels of imaginary coat
9. FAMINE--hold stomach
10. EGYPT--point to far side of room
11. 400 YEARS--hold up four fingers
12. BONDAGE--cross wrists
13. MOSES--hold imaginary staff
14. EXODUS--hold staff over head
15. WANDER IN WILDERNESS--make circles at sides of body, down by hips
16. CONQUEST OF CANAAN--lasso over head
17. JUDGES--hammer fist into palm of other hand
18. KINGS--make crown with hands on top of head
19. UNITED KINGDOM--hold imagined beach ball in front of tummy
20. SAUL --hands gesture "no" down towards floor
21. DAVID --fingers make heart shape, using both hands
22. SOLOMON --one hand makes ½ heart shape, using both hands
23. DIVIDED KINGDOM--split the round beach ball in front of tummy
24. JUDAH→BABYLON--slap hip on right side 2x and point far to right
25. ISRAEL→ASSYRIA--slap hip on left side 2x and point far to left
26. 400 YEARS--hold up four fingers
27. SILENCE--head hangs down toward floor
28. CHRIST--cross wrists in front of face
29. CHURCH--make church (steeple) shape with hands
30. JEWS--rub back of head like a Jewish cap
31. GENTILES--point to own chest
32. WORLD--fling arms out wide
33. REVELATION OF THE FUTURE--pretend to hold binoculars; fingers make two holes to look through

Credits: altered from *Walk Thru the Bible*

Bible history one-minute survey: Key words review/practice

1. c _____
2. f _____
3. f _____
4. n _____
5. A _____
6. I _____
7. J _____
8. J _____
9. f _____
10. E _____
11. _____ years
12. b _____
13. M _____
14. E _____
15. w _____ in w _____
16. c _____ of C _____
17. J _____
18. K _____
19. u _____ k _____
20. S _____
21. D _____
22. S _____
23. d _____ k _____
24. J _____ → B
25. I _____ → A
26. _____ years
27. s _____
28. C _____
29. C _____
30. J _____
31. G _____
32. w _____
33. r _____ of the f _____

Bible history one-minute survey: Key words review/practice *(answer page)*

1. creation
2. fall
3. flood
4. nations
5. Abraham
6. Isaac
7. Jacob
8. Joseph
9. famine
10. Egypt
11. 400 years
12. bondage
13. Moses
14. Exodus
15. wander in wilderness
16. conquest of Canaan
17. Judges
18. Kings
19. united kingdom
20. Saul
21. David
22. Solomon
23. divided kingdom
24. Judah → Babylon
25. Israel → Assyria
26. 400 years
27. silence
28. Christ
29. Church
30. Jews
31. Gentiles
32. world
33. revelation of the future

Lesson 28: The Old Testament books

Historical	Poetical	Prophetical
Genesis Exodus Leviticus Numbers Deuteronomy	Job Psalms Proverbs Ecclesiastes Song of Solomon	Isaiah Jeremiah Lamentations Ezekiel Daniel

Historical (continued):

Joshua
Judges
Ruth
1 Samuel
2 Samuel
1 Kings
2 Kings
1 Chronicles
2 Chronicles

Prophetical (continued):

Hosea
Joel
Amos
Obadiah
Jonah
Micah
Nahum
Habakkuk
Zephaniah

Historical:

Ezra
Nehemiah
Esther

Prophetical:

Haggai
Zechariah
Malachi

Learn the Old Testament books: Using pictures first

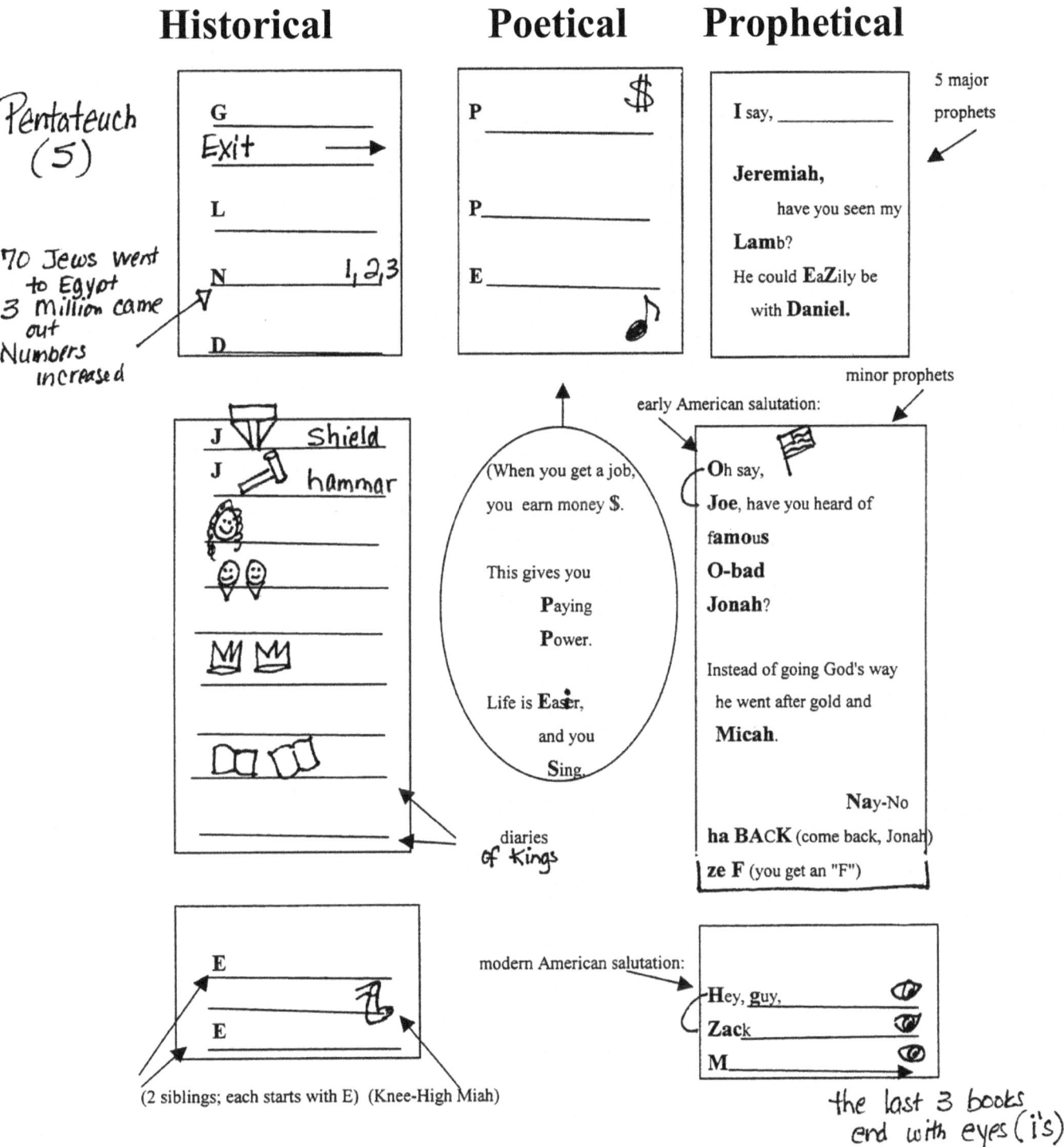

Fill in the pictures and first letters of the names of all the Old Testament books

Unscramble the books

First draw the picture clues, and then list the titles in correct order.

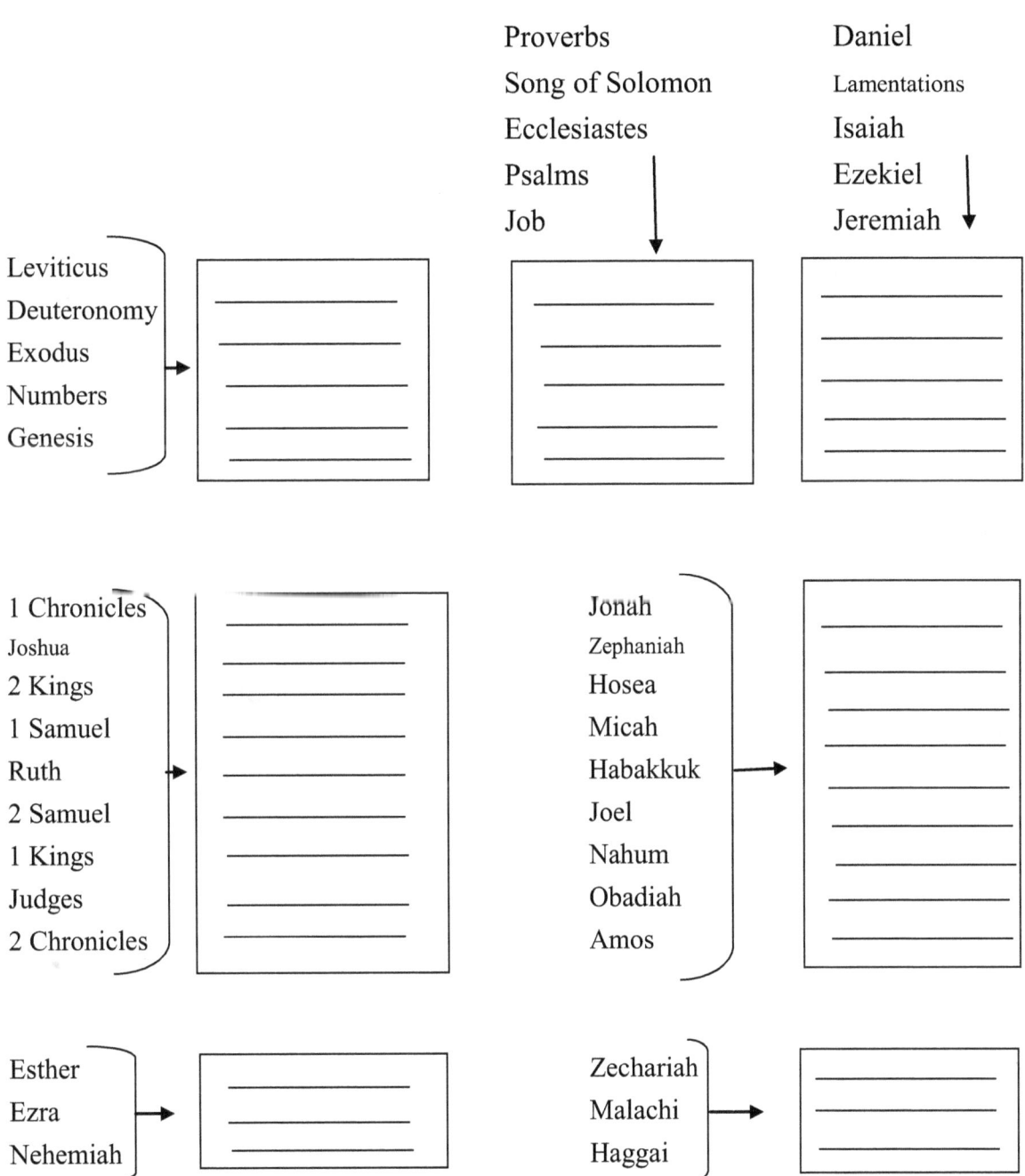

The books, scrambled

Number the Old Testament books in correct order.

_____ Zechariah

__1__ Genesis

_____ Ruth

_____ 2 Kings

_____ Nehemiah

_____ Psalms

_____ Ezekiel

_____ Amos

_____ 2 Chronicles

_____ Numbers

_____ Song of Solomon

_____ Jonah

_____ Malachi

_____ Habakkuk

_____ Joel

_____ Lamentations

_____ Job

_____ 1 Kings

_____ Judges

_____ Leviticus

_____ Joshua

_____ 2 Samuel

_____ Esther

_____ Ecclesiastes

_____ Jeremiah

_____ Hosea

_____ Zephaniah

_____ Exodus

_____ 1 Chronicles

_____ Micah

_____ Haggai

_____ Nahum

_____ Obadiah

_____ Daniel

_____ Isaiah

_____ Proverbs

_____ 1 Samuel

_____ Deuteronomy

_____ Ezra

The books, scrambled *(answer page)*

Here are the Old Testament books, numbered in their correct order.

_38_ Zechariah

_1_ Genesis

_8_ Ruth

_12_ 2 Kings

_16_ Nehemiah

_19_ Psalms

_26_ Ezekiel

_30_ Amos

_14_ 2 Chronicles

_4_ Numbers

_22_ Song of Solomon

_32_ Jonah

_39_ Malachi

_35_ Habakkuk

_29_ Joel

_25_ Lamentations

_18_ Job

_11_ 1 Kings

_7_ Judges

_3_ Leviticus

_6_ Joshua

_10_ 2 Samuel

_17_ Esther

_21_ Ecclesiastes

_24_ Jeremiah

_28_ Hosea

_36_ Zephaniah

_2_ Exodus

_13_ 1 Chronicles

_33_ Micah

_37_ Haggai

_34_ Nahum

_31_ Obadiah

_27_ Daniel

_23_ Isaiah

_20_ Proverbs

_9_ 1 Samuel

_5_ Deuteronomy

_15_ Ezra

The Old Testament books: Final quiz

Now write their names in the appropriate places in the seven boxes.

Lesson 29: New Testament books: Memory hooks

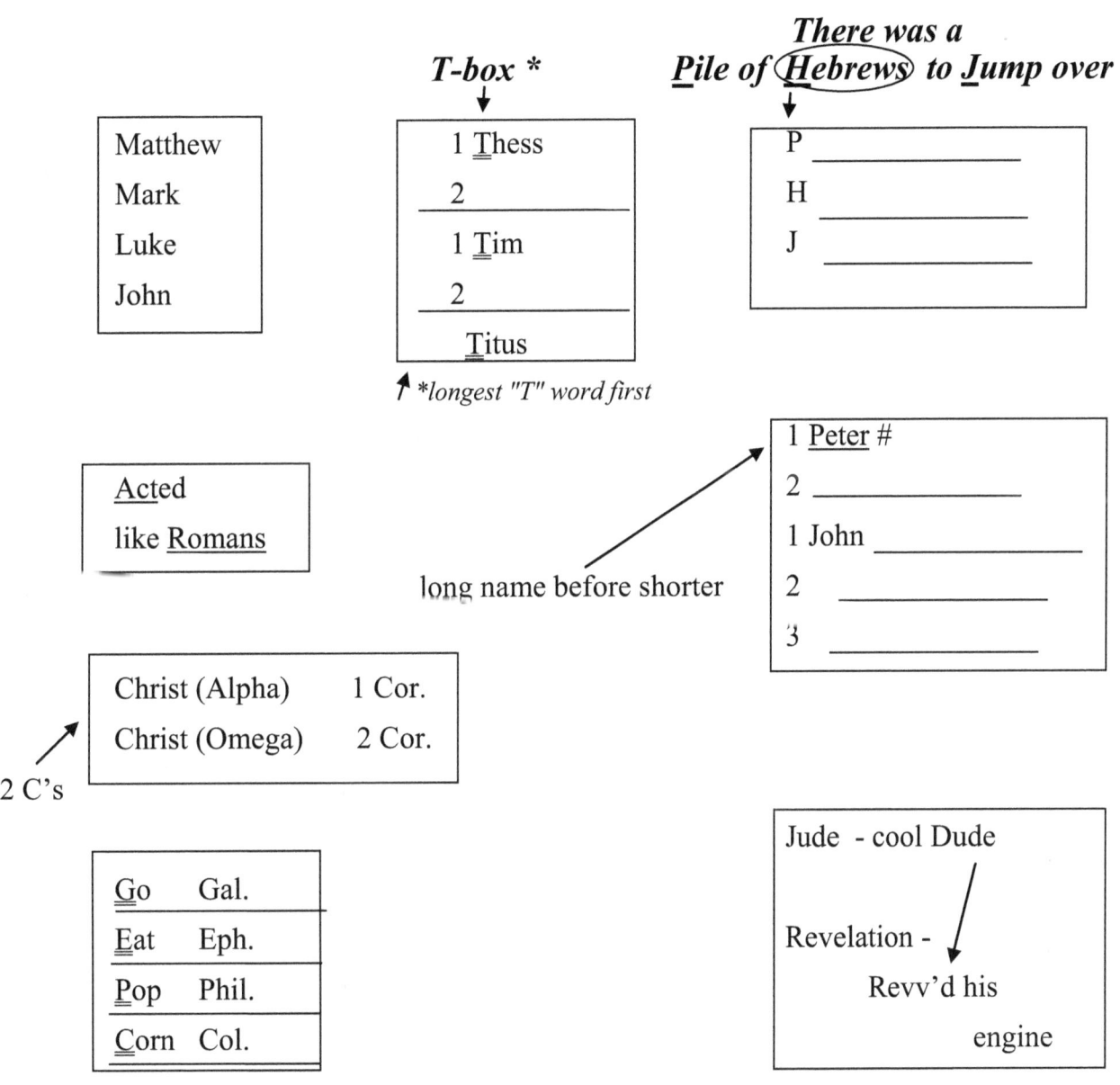

New Testament books (the Apostolic writings)

Write their names in the appropriate places in the eight boxes.

All the books of the Bible *(answer page)*

Old Testament

| Genesis |
| Exodus |
| Leviticus |
| Numbers |
| Deuteronomy |

| Joshua |
| Judges |
| Ruth |
| 1 Samuel |
| 2 Samuel |
| 1 Kings |
| 2 Kings |
| 1 Chronicles |
| 2 Chronicles |

| Ezra |
| Nehemiah |
| Esther |

| Job |
| Psalms |
| Proverbs |
| Ecclesiastes |
| Song of Solomon |

| Isaiah |
| Jeremiah |
| Lamentations |
| Ezekiel |
| Daniel |

| Hosea |
| Joel |
| Amos |
| Obadiah |
| Jonah |
| Micah |
| Nahum |
| Habakkuk |
| Zephaniah |

| Haggai |
| Zechariah |
| Malachi |

New Testament

| Matthew |
| Mark |
| Luke |
| John |

| Acts |
| Romans |

| 1 Corinthians |
| 2 Corinthians |

| Galatians |
| Ephesians |
| Philippians |
| Colossians |

| 1 & 2 Thessalonians |
| 1 & 2 Timothy |
| Titus |

| Philemon |
| Hebrews |
| James |

| 1 & 2 Peter |
| 1, 2 & 3 John |

| Jude |
| Revelation |

Lesson 30: Find a verse in ten seconds

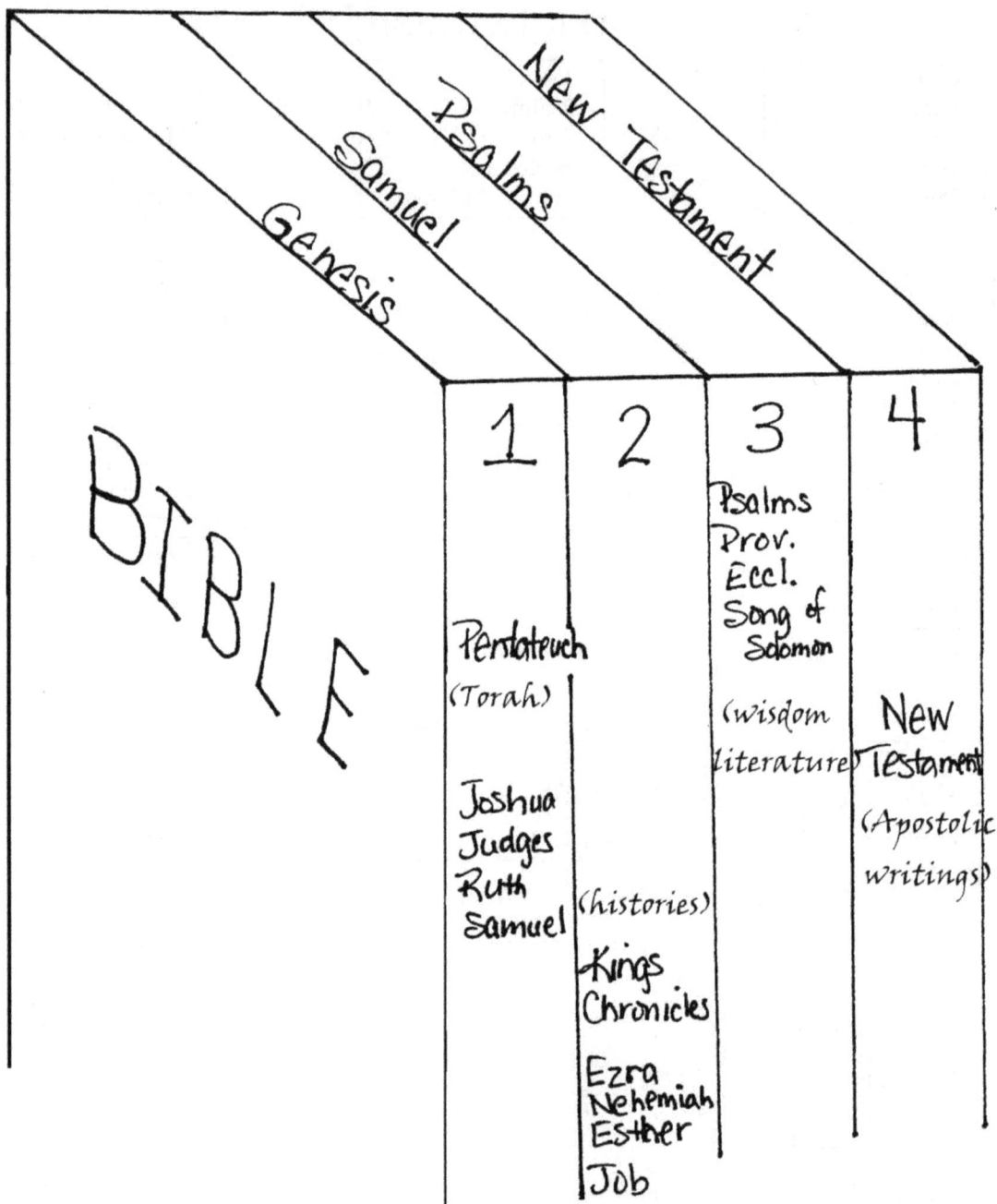

This is one of over 100 practical how-to materials of www.homeschoolhowtos.com (email info@homeschoolhowtos.com)

More resources for child training
at www.homeschoolhowtos.com *For elementary ages & up*

Beyond Discipline: $5.95 in print; $4.95 Kindle; $3.95 e-book
How to train your children, not just discipline them

Practical, loving, nurturing discipline strategies that work. How to run ahead of your children in training and disciplining them. No ho-hum theory here—just teacher-proven, time-tested techniques used with scores of children at the worst times of the day in the worst settings, with happy results.   All of this is included in this book ↓

Teachers' Secrets & Motherhood Savvy for Homeschoolers
(softcover book by Renée Ellison, 236 pages)   **$14.95**   Also available in Kindle format for $9.95

Secrets and **S**avvy for parenting, child training, homeschooling, and home management. Grab these ideas and you'll gain confidence and capability in the place where it matters most—the home. **Topics:**
- The power of a focused mother
- How to *train* your children, not just *discipline* them *(described above)*
- 12 optimal ways to trigger the brain—with any subject matter
- Home management strategies

How to Cultivate a Lasting Love of the Bible in Your Children
(9 pages; #56) **$2.95 print;**
$.99 Kindle or e-book

Six ways to pour the **love** of God's Word into your children, and have them still want more.

Ethel Barrett Tells Bible Stories (audio CD)
(76 minutes; #84)   **$5.99**

Treat your young family to an unforgettable listening experience – resurrected in digital form from LP recordings produced a half century ago. A dozen stories told by "The Story Lady"--one of the most inspirational, popular, and talented Christian personalities in America during the mid-twentieth century. Buy several!

Character Traits Coloring Book & Songs   Color and sing!
For elementary ages (97 pages, with 60 minutes of songs on an audio CD)

Take a break, mom! Your kids can color and sing their way to more noble character. You get 48 "get-you-to-think" coloring pages, 48 "stick-with-you" songs (professionally recorded, with large-print lyrics), and 48 object lessons to drive each point home. Coloring book version choice: NIV or KJV verses.
- ✓ The 97-page coloring book contains pictures of animals and words that actually look and act like the trait they describe! Extra coloring books $8 each.
- ✓ Just the kind of catchy ads you want *your* kids to sing!
- ✓ Get double use of the follow-along song words for character training while your children use them for practicing their typing or penmanship, too.

Training Children Further   **$3.50**
(24 pages; #16)

Ideas for training in subtle areas that most parents just let go. What a difference it can make!

Taken from interviews with families whose children turned out exceptionally well

Dynamite Discipline Strategies for Managing Any Group of Children (DVD)   *(1/2 hour; #95)*   **$6.99**

39 "discipline-how-to's" demonstrated incorrectly by a funny man named Mr. Wrong (Todd) and then is re-done the right way by a different teacher (Renee). Useful for leading a homeschool co-op class, field trip, Sunday school or 4-H class. Viewing this will help you to handle any group of children more easily and confidently. Because the children will be in the palm of your hand, under control, they will really LIKE you, and you'll actually get to move on to LEARNING something together!

This movie was digitized from a vintage recording; it has some background hiss.

HOMESCHOOL HOW-TO'S

Practical helps for homeschooling families

By Renée Ellison

		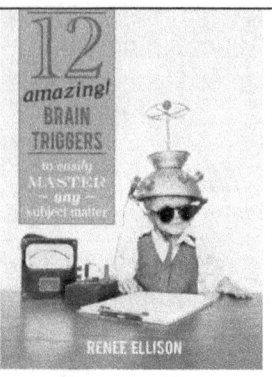	
Preschoolers	Child Training	Teaching	Homeschooling
		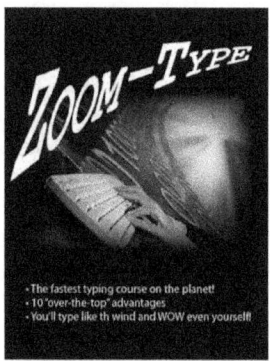	
Character Traits	Piano Course	Touch-typing	Fun Tips

Femininity	Homemaking	Challenges	Special Cases

www.homeschoolhowtos.com   Email: info@homeschoolhowtos.com

Free blogs ~ Kindle/eBooks ~ Homeschool how-to's to give you a boost

www.ingramcontent.com/pod-product-compliance
Lightning Source LLC
Chambersburg PA
CBHW081347040426
42450CB00015B/3337